NORTH CAROLINA RIVERS & CREEKS

· ACKNOWLEDGEMENTS ·

Advertisers

Chattooga Whitewater Outfitters
Diamond Brand Outdoors
Esquif Canoes
Grandfather Mountain
Lendal Paddles
Lotus Designs
Nantahala Outdoor Center
Palm Equipment

Pisgah Whitewater
Power Pawz Hand Paddles
Stahlsac Gear Bags
Sunrift Adventures
Sweet Helmets
Watershed Darybags
Wavesport Kayaks
NRS

North Carolina Rivers & Creeks

ISBN # 9766058-0-5
©2005 Brushy Mountain Publishing, Inc. - all rights reserved.
Edition 1.1. Printed in China.

Contributing Writers

Al Gregory
Ken Strickland
Chris Harjes
Jeb Hall
Trip Kinney
Andria Baldovin
Howard Tidwell
Clay Wright
Bob Pfister
Sutton Bacon
Kevin Colburn

Contributing Photographers

Heath Cowart
Trip Kinney
Melinda Hendershott
JJ Shepherd
Kevin Colburn
Rob Maxwell
Bill Alexander
Dawn Powell
Brit Farthing
Brad Roberts
Victor Jones
John Pruitt
Andria Baldovin
Mark Calcagni
Ryan Bednar
Wayne Dickert
Tom O'Keefe
Matthew Havice
Bryce Yarbrough
Julie Keller
Davis Kessman
Jimmy Nipper
Ben Hayes
Chris Young
Jennifer Petosa
John Parch
Toby McDermott
Jennifer Day Young
Chris Bell
Whetstone Photography
Tommy Hilleke
Teresa Gryder
Brian Sandefur
Gary Dupree
Chris Smith
Chris Bell
Chris McFadden
Dennis Huntley
Sam Drevo

Investors

Ken Driscoll
John Pilson

· INTRO ·

The purchase of a new guidebook, for me, is accompanied by the thrill of all the adventures that the information inside can unfold. Guidebooks have been responsible—at least in part—for both the most incredible adventures and trying epics I have ever been on. This guidebook is no different—it can bring you unforgettable fun filled days on the river, or it can send you into the midst of an ordeal that will give you the willies every time you think about it for years to come. I have made every effort to minimize the chances of the latter, but to increase your odds of avoiding the trip from hell you will need to do three things.

First, be aware that **even the best guidebook is no substitute for good judgement**. This book should be used in combination with a liberal dose of that judgement—both on the river and before you put on. Be honest with yourself about your skills, and make a thorough and objective assessment of the water level, weather, time of day, your group, your equipment, and other factors before putting on the river. This book is simply meant to get you there—only you and your paddling partners can get you safely down the river.

Second, this book will only function properly for you if you take the time to learn how to use it. **Please read the section on how to use the book**—it contains information that is critical to the understanding of the wealth of information that is found here. A good guidebook is like a rescue PFD—incredibly handy, but only safe to use with proper training. Take the time to learn how to get the most from this book.

Third, remember that **rivers are constantly changing**. Although I have made every effort to include the best information available on these streams right now, floods move boulders, storms move wood, and gauges change constantly. It's always a good idea to check with locals or the nccreeks.com website to get the latest info on a run before heading out. Once on the river, exercise caution and realize that this or any guidebook is no substitute for scouting and common sense.

I want to take this opportunity to thank all of the people who have helped with this project—through sending pictures, writing descriptions, or sharing information with me. This is a project brought together by an entire community. I also want to thank the companies and stores who stepped up to support this project and the local boating community through their advertising, and the investors who believed in the project enough to kick in as well—without their help this book could never have happened. I hope the readers will return the favor by looking up those companies and stores, and by providing shuttles, refreshments, and good river karma to Ken Driscoll and John Pilson, and all the writers and photographers who helped make this possible when you meet them at the river.

I also want to thank Gordon Banks for the excellent layout job he did on this book. His Colorado book was the inspiration for the project, and he has delivered a work beautiful enough to do justice to the rivers of this area. Without him, this would still be a jumble of disjointed notes and spreadsheets on my hard drive. I'm psyched that I got to have the book designed by the very best!

Finally, I want to thank Andria for her hard work and incredible patience every step of the way—endless phone calls to advertisers, proof reading, putting up with my moods, sound advice, motivating me to get the job done, and being dragged all over creation to shoot photos—not on the rivers she wanted to go to, but on the rivers that I needed photos of. Without her this book never would have come together.

I hope everybody has a happy, safe, and fun time on the water!

Leland

· HOW TO USE THIS BOOK ·

ORGANIZATION

The river reaches and play spots in this book have been broken down into 9 smaller regions to make your trip planning easier. Within each region, drainages are arranged as the water flows, with the reaches higher in the drainage being listed at the beginning and those lower down following in the order that the river gets to them. If you would prefer to see the rivers listed in order of difficulty or drainage area, you can check the alternate listings in the appendix.

Each region has an intro page followed by an overall map of the entire region, complete with a locator map to see where the mapped area is relative to the big picture of the whole book. Regions are usually further broken down into drainages or smaller areas, each with its own map.

MAPS

All of the maps in the book have been constructed to give you the best possible information at a glance while removing the distraction of everything that is not important. They are all to scale, so relative distances on the map will be right in the real world. Although the distances have not been quantified on the maps, they are quantified in the shuttle directions included with each reach.

REACHES & PLAY SPOTS

There are 101 river reaches and play spots listed in this book. The information on each reach is divided into 3 distinct sections.

Beta - All the vital statistics for each run are placed in the beta for quick reference at a glance. This is the first place to look to see if this might be a run you want to try.

Description - The text description of the run makes an effort to tell you the general character of the run, important info like mandatory portages, some danger locations, and any other critical info that might be useful in trying the run. You will usually not find rapid-by-rapid descriptions, nor will you find every detail of a given run. This job of this book is to get you there and equip you with some knowledge, not to remove all thrill of adventure or sense of personal responsibility from your paddling experience.

Directions - Directions for finding the runs and setting shuttle have been included with every reach. The directions are given from a prominent landmark that should be obvious on the maps in this book as well as most commercially available maps. For shortcuts to many of these landmarks from Asheville, check out the common directions section in the appendix.

UNDERSTANDING BETA

Difficulty - The difficulty of the runs in the book has been designated using the international scale of river difficulty. The ratings apply to the run in the middle of the range of recommended levels. Generally, the rivers should be considered somewhat less difficult on the lower end of the range and more difficult at the higher end. On reaches which have one rapid which is uncharacteristically difficult for that run, the rating of the more difficult rapid is given in parentheses following the overall rating for the reach.

Length - The length of each reach is given in miles of river between the put in and take out.

Put In / Take Out - These are the commonly used points of access for each reach. Often, alternate access points are mentioned in the text shuttle directions which are included with each reach.

Elevation - The elevation of the put in and take out have been given for each reach in feet above sea level.

Gradient - The gradient is the amount of feet of elevation lost in each mile of river. This will often be a good alternate indicator of the difficulty of the run. Gradients have been averaged for rivers with no miles over 100 feet per mile, and are broken down by the mile for rivers with any single mile of gradient over 100 feet per mile. On reaches which do not end with a whole number of miles, the actual number of feet dropped in the final fraction of a mile is given—not an average of that gradient over a complete mile.

Drainage Area / Season - For free flowing streams, the drainage areas have been given in square miles. Generally, rivers with smaller drainage areas have smaller river beds, and—assuming even rainfall over the entire area—require more rain to run, and drop out more quickly after the rain stops. Rivers with larger drainage areas often need less rainfall to get them going, and are more likely to be too high to run after a very heavy rainfall. For rivers that are dam controlled, the season of dam releases has been listed instead of the drainage area.

Gauge - This indicates the best gauge to use to determine if a given reach is running. Often there is more than one indicator for a run, and all of the best indicators have been listed where possible.

Common Gauges

Here are some of the common gauges referred to in the book:

- USGS Streamflows
  NC - http://waterdata.usgs.gov/nc/nwis/current?type=flow
  TN - http://waterdata.usgs.gov/tn/nwis/current?type=flow
  GA - http://waterdata.usgs.gov/ga/nwis/current/?type=flow

- TVA Streamflows
  1-800-238-2264 x3
  http://lakeinfo.tva.gov/htbin/streaminfo

- AFWS Rainfall Data - if you click on the county names there are also some stream flows listed.
  NC - http://www.afws.net/data/nc/ncdata.htm
  TN - http://www.afws.net/data/tn/tndata.htm

- Green River Release Schedule & Lake Level
  Release: 1-800-829-5253 x1,4,2 or 828-698-2068
  Lake Level: 1-800-829-5253 x1,4,1

Other Online Resources

NCCREEKS.com - The website that goes hand in hand with this book! This site has links to all of the flow pages, and the most current information on all of the runs in the book. Please check the website before planning a trip to see if anything has changed on the rivers you're heading for. Also, please stop by and let me know if you find anything that is different than what I've written.

http://www.nccreeks.com/

BOATINGBETA.com - Chris Bell also has an excellent site with flows and interpretation for the region, as well as virtual gauges for several reaches that do not currently have online gauges.

http://boatingbeta.com/cgi-bin/myflows.pl?view

AMERICAN WHITEWATER - Everyone should be an AW member! Along with their incredible work protecting rivers and our access to them, AW has developed an amazing resource on the web—with all sorts of information on most of the rivers in the country.

http://americanwhitewater.org/

Levels - These are the recommended runable levels for each reach. Rivers can certainly be scraped down lower by those willing to sacrifice some plastic, and also can be run higher by folks who want more challenge from a given reach. It is important to remember that unless the gauge is actually measuring the level on the reach in question, these levels are only a guide—not a guarantee that you will find the right levels when you arrive at the river. Always use your best judgement to visually assess the level before putting on the river.

DOGHOBBLE

RHODO

Located in one of the most biologically diverse areas of the country, the mountains of the southern Appalachians are covered with a thick blanket of temperate rainforest. While this rainforest is a treasure that is amazing to behold, it is far from the easiest ecosystem to portage through. You won't be noticing much diversity as you thrash about in the dense vegetation that lines most of the streams here—you will be clawing and cussing as you fight your way through three of the most common and troublesome species to boaters—Rhododendron, Doghobble, and the ever lovable Greenbrier. As you shred your paddling pants and any small piece of exposed skin, keep in mind that if not for these wonderful plants, the banks of the rivers would be much more crowded, and there would be little feel of wilderness left in this populated part of the country.

· FLOODS ·

epic chattooga logjam - ©LD

Rivers are constantly changing. In the southern Appalachians, the primary mode of change is flooding—large pulses of water that come down the river and move rocks, wood, and sediment to new and sometimes exciting locations. It's Mother Nature's house, and she can redecorate the living room any time she likes. Sometimes these little rearrangements are good for whitewater paddling—eliminating portages and opening new lines—and sometimes they can ruin your favorite rapids or play spots. No matter what the outcome, they always require that you keep your eyes open and proceed with caution on the river. Things will not always be the same way as you left them your last time through, and the best policy is always to get out and look.

highway 215 washout after hurricanes frances and ivan - ©LD

Another thing to keep in mind is that one person's playground is another person's disaster area. Many of the days that we rush out to run the goods are the same days that many people have lost all of their goods to the river. No matter what your feelings are on the topic of development on a flood plain, the best policy for maintaining good boater—local relations is to be sensitive to the loss that people have experienced, since many times they will view your paddling the flood waters as having a good time at their expense. It is better to skip a given river and come back another day than to put on and ruin access entirely.

watch for highways and forests in the river - ©LD

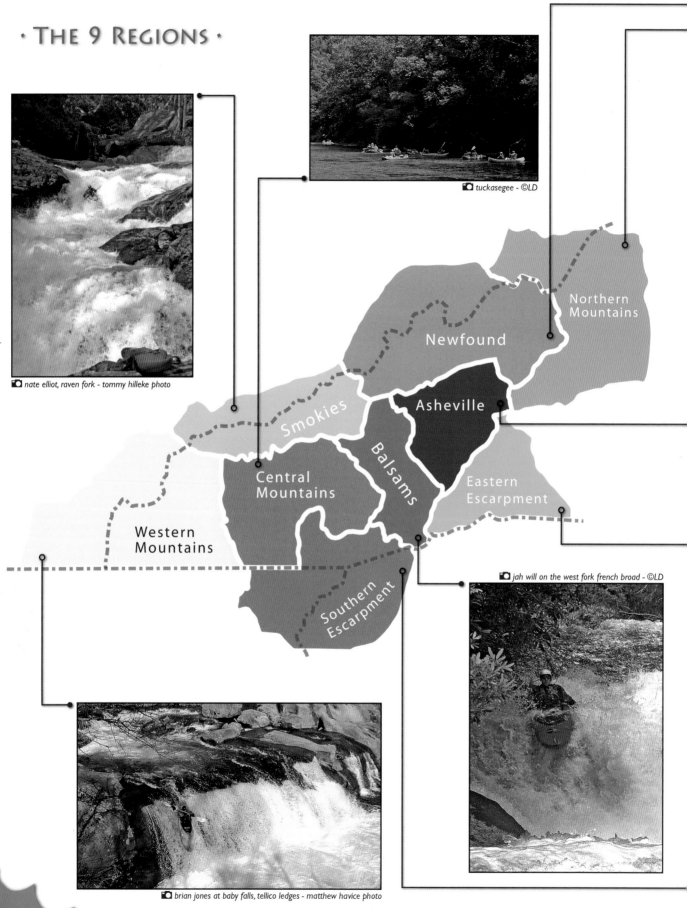

tuckasegee - ©LD

nate elliot, raven fork - tommy hilleke photo

Northern
Mountains

Newfound

Smokies

Asheville

Balsams

Central
Mountains

Eastern
Escarpment

Western
Mountains

Southern
Escarpment

jah will on the west fork french broad - ©LD

brian jones at baby falls, tellico ledges - matthew havice photo

📷 *andria on dragstrip, gragg prong - ©LD*

📷 *john pilson runs the narrows, big laurel - ©LD*

📷 *trafford mcrae at alexander wave - ©LD*

📷 *pat miljour in the groove tube, green narrows - trip kinney photo*

📷 *brent meadows on the warmup ledge, horsepasture river - ©LD*

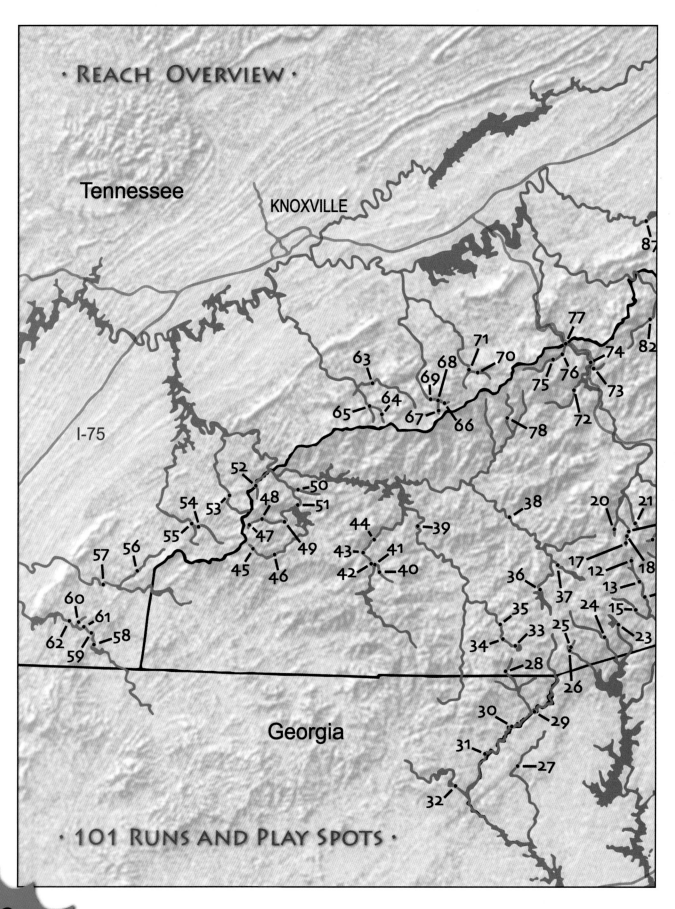

Tennessee

KNOXVILLE

I-75

Georgia

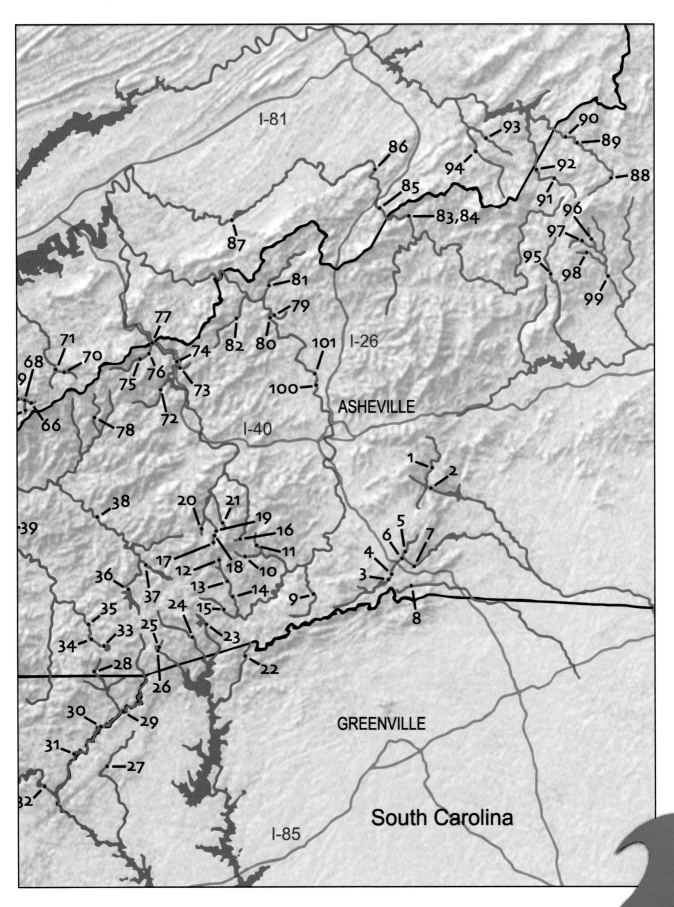

I-81

86

85

93

90

89

94

92

88

83,84

91

96

87

97

95

81

98

79

99

I-26

77

74

82

80

101

71

70

100

68

75

76

73

ASHEVILLE

9

66

78

72

38

I-40

1

I-39

20

21

2

19

16

5

11

6

7

17

12

18

4

10

36

13

3

37

14

9

35

24

15

8

33

25

23

34

28

22

26

30

29

GREENVILLE

31

27

32

South Carolina

I-85

· TOC ·

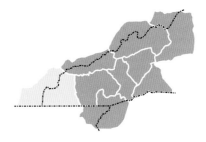

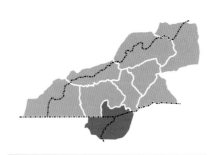

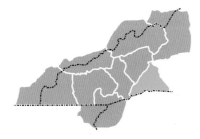

Western Mountains — 119

Eastern Escarpment — 33

Southern Escarpment — 67

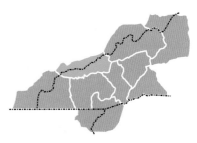

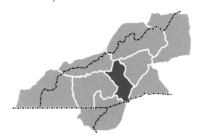

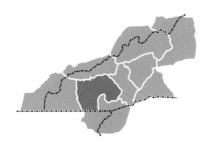

The Balsams — 49

Central Mountains — 103

The Smokies — 145

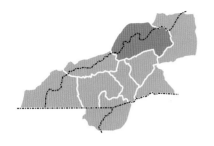

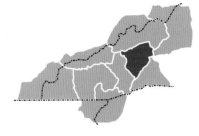

Photo Gallery

robert peerson finishing boof or consequence, green river narrows - sam drevo photo

west fork pigeon tributary - © LD

 *(opposite) scouting the mini-gorge, upper whitewater river - tommy hilleke photo*

 *land bridge portage on the toxaway - tommy hilleke photo*

amos shuman on the highway to heaven, horsepasture river - © LD

andria baldovin on thrasher pike ramp b, horsepasture river - © LD

📷 chris harjes on the horsepasture - © LD

📷 *james witkiewicz in corkscrew, chattooga section IV - © LD*

📷 *(opposite) oceana and the gauntlet from above, tallulah gorge - © rob maxwell*

nate elliot snake charming in anaconda, raven fork - tommy hilleke photo

riley cathcart boofing caveman, raven fork - tommy hilleke photo

the author feeling small in mike tyson's punchout, raven fork - teresa gryder photo

EASTERN
ESCARPMENT

pablo perez at gorilla - ©LD

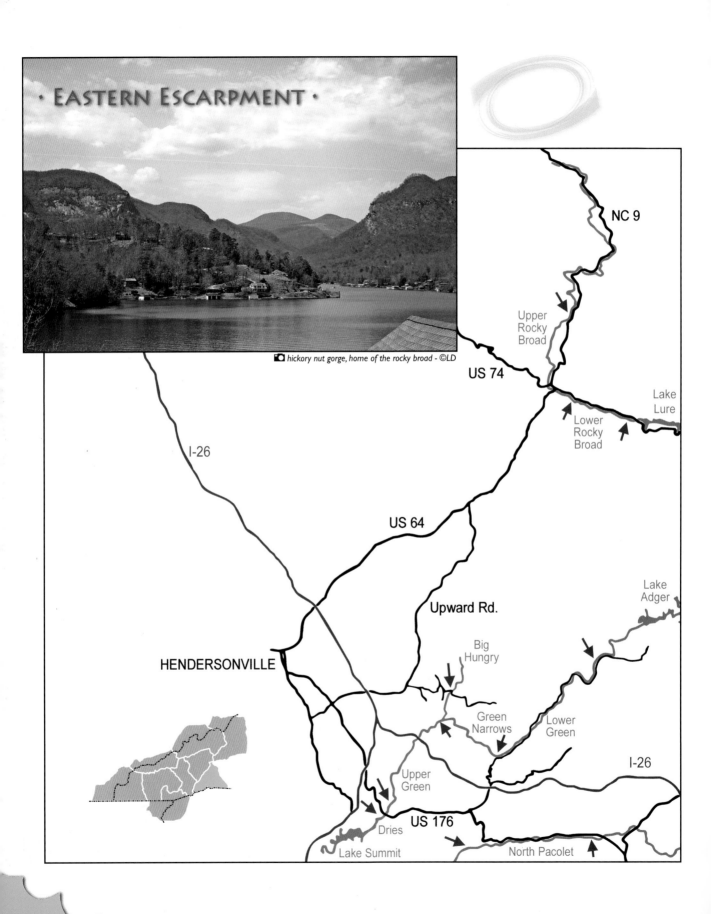

· EASTERN ESCARPMENT ·

hickory nut gorge, home of the rocky broad - ©LD

NC 9

Upper
Rocky
Broad

US 74

Lake
Lure

Lower
Rocky
Broad

I-26

US 64

Lake
Adger

Upward Rd.

Big
Hungry

HENDERSONVILLE

Green
Narrows

Lower
Green

I-26

Upper
Green

US 176

Dries

North Pacolet

Lake Summit

upper rocky broad air - paddler paul bartholic - © LD

DIFFICULTY	V-
LENGTH	4.6 miles
PUT-IN	Flat Creek Road (SSR 2802)
TAKE-OUT	Chimney Rock Welcome Sign
ELEVATION	1957 to 1362
GRADIENT	164,136,120,77,98
DRAINAGE	23 sq. mi.
GAUGE	US 64 Bridge / AFWS Bat Cave SG
LEVELS	4.3' / 4.75' +

BETA

1 · UPPER ROCKY BROAD ·

If the rain is heavy on the east side of Asheville, and you have limited time to get a run in, the Upper Rocky Broad offers some big easy drops and beautiful scenery 40 minutes from town.   Access is delicate on both ends and in the middle, so the motto for this run is "tread lightly." Try your best to be respectful of the no parking and trespassing signs at the put in, and remember to park your car on the east side of highway 9 on the wide grassy spot about 100 yards north of Flat Creek Road. You can slide into the creek from the edge of Flat Creek Road next to the bridge. Be aware that this entire run passes through private property.

The river starts out as a flat stream winding gently through farmland, and if not for the steep ride to the put in you might find yourself wishing you had brought a tube and a cooler along—don't be fooled! Not far into the run, the gorge walls close in and the bottom drops out—sending the creek cascading over a series of vertical drops and slides. Scout the first horizon line on the right, and then make your way to the left above the next one to scout the biggest series of drops on the river. The landing of the bottom drop is not visible from this vantage point, so it is highly advisable that someone eddy out river right before the final drop and take a peek in the landing to make sure it's clear of wood.

After the big drops there are a couple of technical rapids, then the difficulty eases to class III and stays that way until one final class IV/V drop just before the river rejoins the highway. Be very wary of wood in the midsection of this run—world class kayaker and US Freestyle Team member Pablo Perez lost his life here in 1998 in a pin under an unseen log in a class III drop.

If the river is high enough to run the URB, the level will be prime for continuing on down the Lower Rocky Broad if you have the time and the skills.

Shuttle: From Asheville, head east on US 74 over the mountain and down to Bat Cave. In Bat Cave, head left on highway 9 for 3.6 miles and pull out on the grassy shoulder on the right just after passing Flat Creek Road on the left. Walk back down the road a bit to Flat Creek Rd. and use that to access the river, being careful to avoid private property along the road. For the put in, return to 74 / 64 and continue east less than a mile past the US 64 bridge over the river to the Chimney Rock welcome sign. DO NOT PARK AT THE CIDER PLACE AT THE US 64 BRIDGE, OR ANYWHERE AROUND THERE. There have been many problems with local land and business owners in the past.

📷 *(above) paddler andria baldovin - © LD*

BETA	
DIFFICULTY	V
LENGTH	2.3 miles
PUT-IN	Chimney Rock Welcome Sign
TAKE-OUT	Riverside Park
ELEVATION	1362 to 1024
GRADIENT	188, 133, 17
DRAINAGE	64.4 sq. mi.
GAUGE	US 64 / AFWS Bat Cave SG
LEVELS	3.8'+ / 4.3'+

2 · LOWER ROCKY BROAD ·

Formerly a staple on the Asheville creek boating menu, this run has enjoyed relative obscurity since 1996. Before that time, the Rocky Broad ran almost every day from November through April, and local boaters would meet at the put in—just 35 minutes from Asheville—every Tuesday afternoon for a run.

On September 5th, 1996, 12 inches of rain fell on the drainage's 3 equal sized tributaries in 3 hours, sending a 30 foot wall of water through the gorge destroying bridges, homes, businesses, and tumbling boulders the size of buses around in the river bed. Driving through shortly after the flood I was shocked to see whole trees wedged horizontally 30 feet up in the branches of their surviving brethren. What resulted was the destruction of some great rapids, creation of some new ones, and dechannelization of the river bed which has left the river runnable only after a pretty good rain.

When you can catch it with water, this river boasts some fantastic class IV/V boulder garden slots and boofs—created by chunks of rock fallen into the river bed from the towering walls of Hickory Nut Gorge 1500 feet above. Despite the adjacent highway, agricultural brown water, post-flood riverbed rubble, and tourist trap aura of the valley, this creek actually boasts some fantastic scenery—a testament to how absolutely spectacular the place must have been before the highway brought in the gift shops, bed and breakfasts and bar-b-que joints. Despite the urban jungle atmosphere, boaters who are careful of wood and other debris will find a great run in Hickory Nut Gorge.

Shuttle: From Asheville, head east on US 74 over the mountain and down to Bat Cave. The put in is less than a mile past the US 64 bridge over the river at the Chimney Rock welcome sign. DO NOT PARK AT THE CIDER PLACE AT THE BRIDGE, OR ANYWHERE AROUND THERE. There have been many problems with local land and business owners in the past. For the take out, continue downstream through the town of Chimney Rock and park at the small park on the right just past the center of town.

• Green River Drainage •

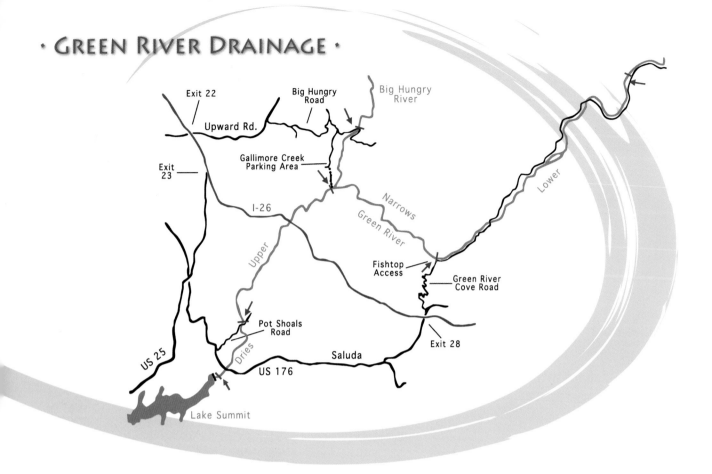

Flows: The flows on the Upper, Narrows, and Lower sections of the Green are determined by the releases from Duke Power's Tuxedo Hydro Plant upstream. Unlike most other hydro plants, the Green has a win-win situation since the river flows when the plant generates power, instead of being dewatered when generation occurs. Due to this and a wet drainage, the Green runs about 80% of the time. The releases are determined every morning and updated to a voice recording that you can get by calling the Duke Power Lake Neighbor Information Line—usually any time after 8 AM.

To get the day's release dial 1-800-829-5253 and select choices 1, 4, and 2. If you want to skip the menus and dial direct, the number is 828-698-2068.

If it's been raining, there could be some natural flow into the Green as well. Flow over the dam can be a factor for all sections. To find out if water is flowing over the dam, dial the 1-800-829-5253 line and select 1, 4, 1. This will give you the lake level in feet, with 100 feet being a full lake. If the level is greater than 100 feet, subtract 100 from the reading to get the number of feet of water coming over the dam. The dam is quite wide, so it doesn't take much water coming over to raise the flow considerably. This is also how you determine if there is water flowing into the Dries section. Even if the lake is not full, there can be extra flow in the Narrows and Lower sections from the Big Hungry River, so use caution if it's been raining lately.

Gallimore Creek Parking: Parking for the access point at the bottom of the Upper / top of the Narrows has been a delicate situation for some time now. As of the writing of this book, some very kind local landowners have leased a piece of property to a group of paddlers for a parking area off of Gallimore Road. Due to paddlers not adhering to the honor system, the gate to the parking lot is kept locked and is only accessible by either purchasing a key or finding a key holder to let you in and out and then paying the daily use fee. Keys can be purchased for $60 per year. Contact Woody at Liquid Logic to find out how you can get one—828-698-5778. Please respect this agreement and do not drive around or damage the gate, as that could cost us all access.

DO NOT PARK IN THE HUNTER PARKING SPACES ACROSS FROM THE LOT. These spaces are reserved for people using the gamelands for hunting and fishing. Parking here can result in a tow, as well as in the agitation of the landowners who lease us the property and the managers of the gamelands.

Please be sure to observe a speed limit of 20 mph on Gallimore Road—there are local residents who use the road, and there have been many close calls from people driving too fast on this road.

3 · GREEN RIVER DRIES ·

DIFFICULTY	IV+
LENGTH	1.35 miles
PUT-IN	Summit Dam
TAKE-OUT	Tuxedo Hydro Plant
ELEVATION	1906 to 1715
GRADIENT	159,32
DRAINAGE	42.4 sq. mi.
GAUGE	1-800-829-5253-1-4-1
LEVELS	100.5 - 101 ft.

BETA

📷 water spills over summit dam   © LD

In the early days of Green Narrows runs, this section was the put in for the entire stretch, which went from the dam all the way to Fishtop Access. At that time, technical problems at the power plant prevented generation, necessitating the release of water through the spillway tubes at the dam. Today, the power plant is back online—diverting the water through the flumes and into the river at the put in for the Upper, and the Dries can only be caught after a pretty good rain brings the water up to where the flume can't hold it all. When this happens, water spills over the dam and into the Dries, opening up the opportunity for an excellent class IV+ run which is a step up from the Upper and a step down from the Narrows.

Putting in at the base of the dam, float through some easier water until you see the old bridge high above you, being aware of the dam construction and lake rubble which can litter the riverbed. Under the bridge the action starts with two slides that can develop some sticky holes at higher water. Below this, the river switches gears to boulder gardens, winding to the left of an island. At the bottom of this stretch is the final hoorah—two larger drops ending in Powerhouse Falls, which is visible from the take out road. Overall, this run offers some great rapids if you don't mind dodging a little dam rubble.

Shuttle: To reach the take out, take exit 54 from I-26 and follow the connector a little over 1.5 miles to the exit at US 176. Take 176 East toward Saluda 1.9 miles to Pot Shoals Road on the left. Follow Pot Shoals down the hill and across the river, and park in the lot immediately across the bridge on the left. To get to the put in, head back up Pot Shoals and continue east across the bridge over the Green, parking in the parking area on the right just past the bridge. Carry back across the bridge, and scramble down to the flume on river left. Follow the flume upstream, scrambling down to put in just downstream of the base of the dam.

📷 powerhouse falls - paddler chris young

4 · UPPER GREEN ·

DIFFICULTY	II+ (III+)
LENGTH	3.75 miles
PUT-IN	Power Plant
TAKE-OUT	Big Hungry Creek
ELEVATION	1715 to 1557
GRADIENT	42 fpm
DRAINAGE	Dam Release
GAUGE	1-800-829-5253-1-4-2
LEVELS	100% - 200%

BETA

With beautiful scenery, reasonable access, and reliable releases year round, this run has established itself as one of the premiere class II/III+ resources of the southeast over the last ten years. With numerous class II rapids and two large class III+ rapids, the Upper Green may well be the perfect introduction to creeking for early intermediate paddlers—except for the walk up the hill at the end.

Putting in just downstream of the bridge below the powerhouse, paddlers will find some fun class II for the first 3/4 mile. A loud roar and a distinct horizon line signal time for a scout at Bayless' Boof. Scout and run (or walk) the left side of the left channel, being wary of a piton rock hidden in the foam at the base of the drop. About 100 yards downstream is a 3 foot slab into Wanda's hole—the stickiest spot on the run, which can be run right or left.

After another 2 miles of class II, the river passes under the towering I-26 bridge. A few bends beyond is pinball, the second of the larger rapids on the run. This one is trickier to scout and walk than Bayless', but can be run fairly easily by simply staying in the main flow off of the double drop angling left. Another 3/4 mile will bring you to the two surfing waves that signal the end of the run. Take out on the left about 75 yards below these waves. If you see Big Hungry entering from the left, you need to get out and walk back upstream unless you're ready for some serious action in the class V Narrows section below. Follow the trail .6 miles uphill to the Gallimore Creek parking area, bearing right when the trail hits the old road.

Shuttle: To reach the put in, take exit 54 from I-26. Follow the connector to a left on hwy 176. Continue 1.9 miles on 176 to Pot Shoals Road on the left. Take Pot shoals road to the parking area just across the river. For the take out, take exit 53 from I-26 (Upward Road). Go east 1.7 miles to a right on Big Hungry Road. After .5 miles, bear left on Big Hungry Road. Bear right .25 miles later on Big Hungry Road. Continue .5 miles to a right on Gallimore Road. Take Gallimore Road .65 miles to Gallimore Creek Parking Area on the Right.

paddler melinda hendershott • © pisgahwhitewater.com

bayless' boof © LD

aiming for the piton rock © LD

5 · BIG HUNGRY ·

'BIG HUNGRY'

DIFFICULTY	IV
LENGTH	1.3 miles
PUT-IN	Big Hungry Road
TAKE-OUT	Green River
ELEVATION	1716 to 1558
GRADIENT	110, 48
DRAINAGE	19.3 sq. mi.
GAUGE	Visual
LEVELS	n/a

BETA

SOUP

twin cheeks - paddler leland - trip kinney photo

After a good rain, Big Hungry is a great alternate way down to the Green Narrows, or a fun class IV creek run in its own right—if you don't mind the walk up the hill at the end. Putting in just below the dam near Big Hungry Road, you will find some small vertical ledges in the first section, followed by a flat area that is actually a small lake. Be careful not to wash into the rubble of the broken down dam at the end of the lake. Portage left, and seal launch back into the river for a run over Big Hungry's largest rapid—Twin Cheeks—named for the bruises left on the asses of the first descenders by the rock hidden in the landing.

Below Twin Cheeks the pace picks up, culminating in the 4 drops of the Hungry Narrows—which begin with a chute on the left beside a large river right boulder. Scout right. Shortly below the Narrows, Big Hungry dumps into the put in for the Green River Narrows, which will be running high on days when Big Hungry is runable and there is a release from Tuxedo Hydro Plant. Tighten your PFD straps and head on downstream if you're up to the challenge, or exit river right on the sandbar at the confluence and head up the trail .6 miles to the Gallimore Creek parking area.

Shuttle: To reach the take out, take exit 53 from I-26 (Upward Road). Go east 1.7 miles to a right on Big Hungry Road. After .5 miles, bear left on Big Hungry Road. Bear right .25 miles later on Big Hungry Road. Continue .5 miles to a right on Gallimore Road. Take Gallimore Road .65 miles to Gallimore Creek Parking Area on the Right. For the put in, return to Big Hungry Road and go right. Park just before the bridge over the Big Hungry River.

kevin colburn in the narrows - © LD

6 · GREEN NARROWS ·

frankenstein - paddler kevin colburn - trip kinney photo

DIFFICULTY	V (V+)
LENGTH	2.8 miles
PUT-IN	Gallimore Creek Road
TAKE-OUT	Fishtop Access
ELEVATION	1619 to 1080
GRADIENT	156, 286, 97
DRAINAGE	Dam Release
GAUGE	1-800-829-5253-1-4-2
LEVELS	60% - 200%

BETA

Imagine a super classic class V creek with drops of such high quality and scenery so spectacular that it is certain to be the chosen destination after every rainfall. Then imagine that river with reliable dam release flows over 300 days a year. This is the reality of the mighty Green River Narrows—the standard creek by which most other creeks are measured, and the ultimate training ground of many of the World's finest hair boaters. Whether you're cutting your creeking teeth on the many class IV and V rapids or firing up the "big three" class V+ drops at high water—the Green has what it takes to satisfy discerning gradient lovers when the water isn't flowing anywhere else in the area.

Walk down the hill .6 miles from the parking area and slide into the small stream gurgling through the hemlocks. Passing Big Hungry River on the left, stop to check out the gauge rock sticking out of the pool on river left at the confluence. When water is barely flowing over the top of the rock, you have an optimal "winter 100%". If the water is more than an inch below the top of the rock you're in for a bit of rock bashing, and if it's more than an inch or two over the rock be ready for some juice!

The first 1/2 mile is warmup class II, and when the gorge narrows and the fun begins you'll know it—Bride of Frankenstein signals the start of the gradient. Frankenstein, Pincushion, Boof or Consequence, Go Left and Die, Zwick's Backender, Chief, Pencil Sharpener, the Notch, Gorilla, Green Scream Machine, Nies' Pieces, Power Slide, Rapid Transit, Nutcracker, Groove Tube, Sunshine Falls and more await downstream. Most of the rapids are manageable class IV and easy V—with the exception of the big three: Go Left, Gorilla, and Sunshine. Many of the drops warrant scouting—and it should be noted that there is a deadly sieve hidden in the landing of Chief, and that a swim at Zwick's

often results in your boat bursting as it washes over Gorilla full of water. Four slides below Gorilla, the river dumps into a large pool with a boulder jumble/log jam combo at the end. Get out here for Nutcracker—portaging left to run Groove Tube. Scout carefully before running this drop, as there is a must make eddy below on the right for scouting or walking Sunshine Falls—the final rapid of the inner gorge.

Below Sunshine, the river mellows to class III and IV rapids interspersed with class II shoals for a mile, before it gets in a last thrill at Toilet Bowl and Hammer Factor. Head right of the island after this last class V, running the small drop of Bitchslap and taking out at the beach on the right where the channels converge.

Shuttle: For the put in, take exit 53 from I-26 (Upward Road). Go east 1.7 miles to a right on Big Hungry Road. After .5 miles, bear left on Big Hungry Road. Bear right .25 miles later on Big Hungry Road. Continue .5 miles to a right on Gallimore Road. Take Gallimore Road .65 miles to Gallimore Creek Parking Area on the Right. Cross the road and carry down the orange gated road .6 miles to the river. You will need to bear left onto a small track when the road turns up hill. To reach the take out, take exit 59 from I-26 (Saluda exit). Head north (non Texaco side) just past the on-ramp to Green River Cove Road on the left. Take Green River Cove road to Fishtop Access on the left at the bottom of the steep curvy road down the hill.

- sunshine falls - paddler andria baldovin - © LD

- pat miljour enters the groove tube - trip kinney photo

- zwick's backender - paddler pat miljour - trip kinney photo

ben hayes goes left - © LD

7 · LOWER GREEN ·

DIFFICULTY	I/II
LENGTH	6.3 miles
PUT-IN	Fishtop Access
TAKE-OUT	Big Rock Access
ELEVATION	1051 to 919
GRADIENT	21 fpm
DRAINAGE	Dam Release
GAUGE	1-800-829-5253-1-4-2
LEVELS	100% - 200%

BETA

lower green scene - © pisgahwhitewater.com

The Lower Green is the second most traveled section of river in North Carolina—largely because it has reliable water most of the year and is probably the most perfect river in the southeast for a first moving water experience. The class I/II shoals provide an excellent learning ground—with well defined eddies and small chutes perfect for the beginning boater. The access is easy, and the river even has a park and play wave that is great for a first surfing experience.

Put in at the beach at Fishtop and warm up with some ferries and roll practice in the pool. If it's summer, you will spend some time dodging summer camp kayak classes and the numerous tubers, who come from all over the area to rent tubes and catch a tan and a buzz while challenging the rapids of the mighty Lower Green. Head on downstream, facing one of the more difficult rapids right off the bat. If you've made it to the first bridge without swimming, you're probably going to be fine on the lower.

typical lower green river runner - © pisgahwhitewater.com

Other spots of note include the largest rapid—Big Corky, a class II shoals found just upstream of the river left tubing outpost/campground, about 1.5 miles downstream of the first bridge. About a mile below this, at a point where the river comes right next to the road, you will find an excellent little wave, perfect for learning the front surf—with parking spots directly adjacent to it on the road. This spot makes a great short take out, or you can continue through the next rapid, Little Corky, and use another alternate takeout just downstream at the second bridge.

Shuttle: To reach the river, take exit 59 from I-26 (Saluda exit). Head north (non Texaco side) just past the on-ramp to Green River Cove Road on the left. Take Green River Cove road to the put in at Fishtop Access on the left at the bottom of the hill. You can take out anywhere along the river downstream from here to the Big Rock access point in the disgusting clearcut downstream.

lower green surf wave - paddler hope carlson - © pisgahwhitewater.com

• LOWER JOE CREEK •

sliding rock - paddler kevin colburn - © LD

This little gem is a fantastic whitewater resource going to waste right under all of our noses, and there's nothing we can do about it. With a dam that is privately owned and a put in and take out that are both on private land, there is no way to get to the incredible slides that lurk in the rhododendron here, and no way to turn on the water any more. I first cleaned out and ran this creek with Lean Bell in the fall of 1994, and we openend the valves on the dam for several more "whitewater releases" over the next few years. A few dozen paddlers got to enjoy the 100 foot long Suicide Slide, the double slide of Sliding Rock, Cabana Rapid, Tube Run, and the final gauntlet of Bridge Falls into Kissrock into Paddle Snap. In the late 1990s, a change of ownership shut down this little creek for good since the current owner has no interest in opening it up to paddlers even on a limited basis. It will wait for future generations to explore again when the winds of access blow the other way.

paddlesnap - paddler kevin colburn - © LD

kissrock - paddler trip kinney - © LD

Kevin Colburn mid slide on Kissrock - © LD

8 · NORTH PACOLET ·

The North Pacolet is a tiny, rubbly creek which winds down the Saluda Grade along US highway 176 from Saluda to Tryon. Sporting some good gradient and alternating bedrock drops and road blast boulder gardens, this run is probably only interesting if you're a Saluda local jonesing for a quick paddle on a day when the Green is going to be a little bit too high, or a homesick Colorado boater looking for some familiar road blast. Be on the lookout for wood and sieves, as both are found in abundance on this trashy run that does have a few fun drops mixed in.

Shuttle: To reach the put in, take exit 59 (Saluda Exit) from I-26. Head toward Saluda (Texaco side of exit) until you intersect with US 176. Turn left on 176, and go 2.6 miles down to a right turn which goes down along the river. Drive upstream to the bridge, cross the river, and continue upstream to the Pearson's Falls Parking Lot. To reach the takeout, drive downstream on 176 until you find a spot that looks good.

© LD

BETA	
DIFFICULTY	IV/V
LENGTH	2 miles
PUT-IN	Pearson Falls Parking
TAKE-OUT	roadside
ELEVATION	1531 to 1162
GRADIENT	93,276
DRAINAGE	9 sq. mi.
GAUGE	Visual
LEVELS	n/a

9 · DUPONT ·

Since the formation of the Dupont State Forest and the opening of the forest to paddling, the drops on the Little River have become a park & huck oasis for Hendersonville and Brevard area paddlers. Triple Falls boasts three giant class V drops, with the middle one being the most runable of the three, and the bottom one being the most dangerous. Downstream of the Dupont Road bridge, Hooker Falls offers a fairly clean 15 foot drop into a big pool—suitable for boaters who don't yet have the skills for Triple Falls. The Little is a fairly large river with a huge drainage, making these drops runable on lots of days when the other Brevard area creeks are a bit too low.

Don't forget to take your mountain bike with you if you head this way. Dupont is home to some of the finest trails in the east, and boasts the best slickrock riding this side of Utah.

Shuttle: From the 64/280/276 junction in Pisgah Forest (near Brevard) drive 3.7 miles East on US 64 to a right on Little River Rd. at the Triangle stop across from Penrose Quarry. Continue 4.2 miles on Little River Rd. to a right on Dupont Rd. The parking area is just before the bridge over the river, about 3 miles up Dupont Rd. Follow the well marked trails upstream to Triple Falls or downstream to Hooker Falls.

DIFFICULTY	V+
LENGTH	.8 miles
PUT-IN	Triple Falls
TAKE-OUT	Hooker Falls
ELEVATION	2395 to 2241
GRADIENT	154 (121 ft in .1 miles)
DRAINAGE	32.9 sq. mi.
GAUGE	Visual
LEVELS	n/a

BETA

AMERICAN AW WHITEWATER

hooker falls - paddler leland - kevin colburn photo

triple falls - paddler tommy hilleke - jj shepherd photo

THE
BALSAMS

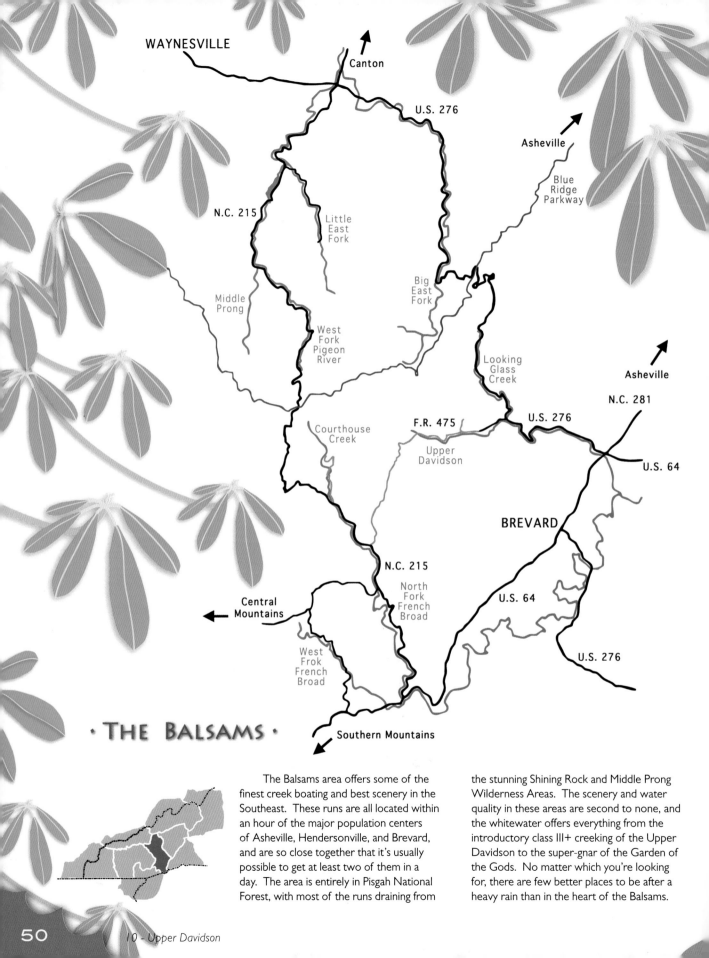

WAYNESVILLE

Canton

U.S. 276

Asheville

Blue Ridge Parkway

N.C. 215

Little East Fork

Middle Prong

Big East Fork

West Fork Pigeon River

Looking Glass Creek

Asheville

N.C. 281

Courthouse Creek

F.R. 475

U.S. 276

U.S. 64

Upper Davidson

BREVARD

N.C. 215

North Fork French Broad

U.S. 64

Central Mountains

West Frok French Broad

U.S. 276

· THE BALSAMS ·

Southern Mountains

The Balsams area offers some of the finest creek boating and best scenery in the Southeast. These runs are all located within an hour of the major population centers of Asheville, Hendersonville, and Brevard, and are so close together that it's usually possible to get at least two of them in a day. The area is entirely in Pisgah National Forest, with most of the runs draining from the stunning Shining Rock and Middle Prong Wilderness Areas. The scenery and water quality in these areas are second to none, and the whitewater offers everything from the introductory class III+ creeking of the Upper Davidson to the super-gnar of the Garden of the Gods. No matter which you're looking for, there are few better places to be after a heavy rain than in the heart of the Balsams.

10 · UPPER DAVIDSON ·

BETA		
DIFFICULTY	II/III (IV)	
LENGTH	1.25 miles	
PUT-IN	Cove Creek	
TAKE-OUT	Above Low Head Dam	
ELEVATION	2519 to 2369	
GRADIENT	118, 32	
DRAINAGE	11.2 sq. mi.	
GAUGE	Davidson 64 Gauge	
LEVELS	2' - 4'	

The Upper Davidson is a favorite rainy afternoon jaunt for creekers from the Brevard area—but remains fairly hard to catch with water for those who live farther away. It's always a good bet if you head to the North Fork of the French Broad and find it too high. Set in a beautiful mountain setting and never straying more than a few hundred yards from the road, the Davidson is a great place for intermediate boaters to try their hands at micro creeking in an intimate rhododendron corridor.

The largest rapid, Whalesback, is found right at the put in at the confluence of the Davidson and Cove Creek. There are two more drops of consequence downstream which might warrant scouting as well. The main obstacle of importance, however, is the low head dam at the takeout—you want to carefully scout this from the road on the way up and make sure that you get out before it. It is located about 100 yards upstream of the fork in the dirt road just beyond the fish hatchery. Although it is usually class III+ in character, this run can pump up to a solid class IV at levels above 4', with huge holes, very fast moving water, and a serious reduction in the number of eddies.

Whether you go high or low, be on the lookout for wood in this tiny stream, and enjoy the ear to ear grin you'll have on your drive back up for your second run.

Note: for a fun multi-sport day, you can mountain bike your shuttle on Davidson River Trail. Bear left around a brown gate just upstream of the low head dam to hit the trail.

Gauge: The gauge is located on river right about 30 yards upstream of the US 64 bridge over the Davidson near the 64/276/280 junction.

Shuttle: from the 64/276/280 junction at Pisgah Forest (near Brevard), drive north into Pisgah on 276 a little over 5 miles to a left turn on FR 475. Follow 475 past the fish hatchery and pull out upstream of the low head dam for the take out. To reach the put in, continue on 475 to the pull out on the left near the entrance to the Cove Creek rec area.

📷 *low head dam at low water as seen from the road © LD*

📷 © LD

11 · LOOKING GLASS CREEK ·

DIFFICULTY	IV/V
LENGTH	.4 miles
PUT-IN	second pullout below sliding rock
TAKE-OUT	next pullout down
ELEVATION	2646 to 2520
GRADIENT	126
DRAINAGE	6.9 sq. mi.
GAUGE	Davidson 64 Gauge / Looking Glass Creek Gauge
LEVELS	3'+ / 1.4' - 2.0'

Looking Glass Creek is a much over-looked stream in an area with plenty of whitewater to offer. When most people think of Looking Glass, they think of the falls—a 55 foot roadside drop that is far downstream of the regular run, and has only seen 4 runs—with mixed results. The regular Looking Glass run is a small stream with many fun rapids, and once the lines are learned it's a great place to do laps as the water quickly drops.

The action starts at one of the designated fun spots in Pisgah, Sliding Rock. Use caution in the summer months because the natural water slide is packed with other non-kayaking fun seekers—and a lower put in might be in order. Normally when the water is high enough to kayak, the swimmers are absent. For your convenience, there is a viewing platform to scout from. After this rapid is a short shallow bedrock section that transitions directly into another clean slide that is slightly bigger than the first with potential rhododendron interference from the right. It is recommended to start middle and stay middle. Downstream there are a couple of intermediate drops before the intimidating horizon line of Triple Drop. If you didn't do the pre-run roadside scout, getting out on the left to have a look is encouraged, as this drop leads directly into the next three small technical rapids.

Below Triple Drop the character of the creek changes from ultra clean bedrock to small technical bouldery drops. There are six to eight places you need to know the line. These drops are extremely fun—ranging from multi-tiered technical to straight six and eight foot boofs. There is an abundance of overhanging trees and rhododendron. The river will get flat and rocky 100 feet after the last class 3 drop. As soon as the gradient ends look for the two large trees growing on the left bank creating eddies on the outside of a right hand bend. Take out here and hike up to the road. Take the time to get to know this run before putting on—things happen fast, and once familiar bombing down is really exciting.

The visual gauge should be checked before the run. It is located above Looking Glass Falls just before the next pull-out. The gauge is mounted to a cement channel barrier on river right.

Al Gregory

Shuttle: From the 276/280/64 junction in Pisgah Forest (near Brevard) head into Pisgah on US 276 about 7.5 miles to Sliding Rock. Turn around, and park in the first available pullout downstream of the Sliding Rock entrance. Put in here and walk the shuttle, or leave a shuttle vehicle .5 miles downstream.

triple drop - paddler al gregory - photo jj shepherd

📷 corran addison on the first descent of looking glass falls, 11/89

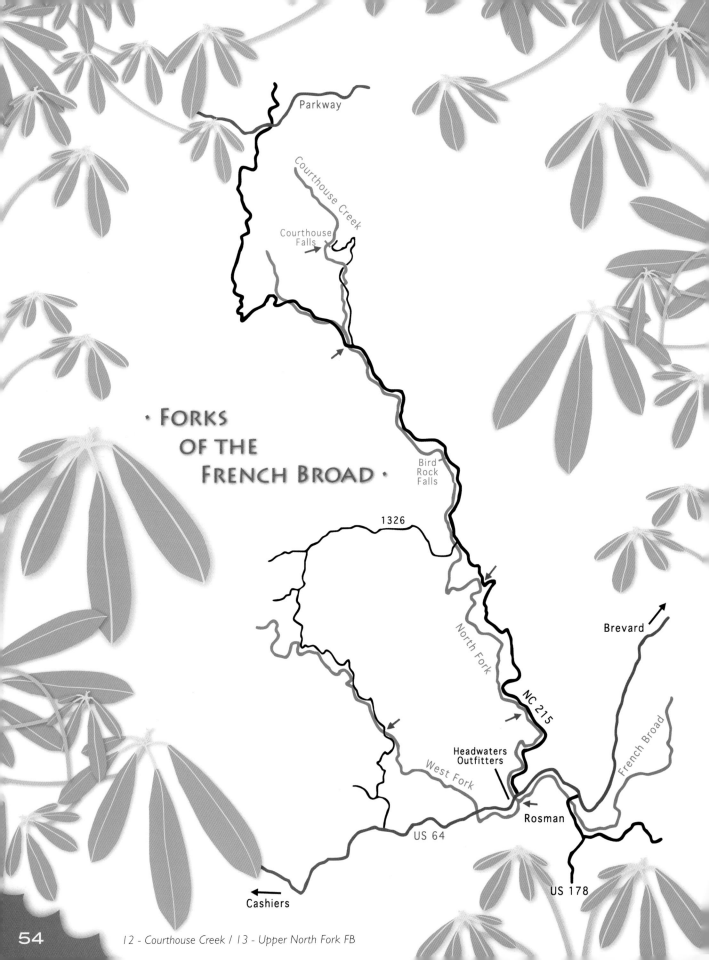

FORKS
OF THE
FRENCH BROAD

Parkway

Courthouse Creek

Courthouse Falls

Bird Rock Falls

1326

North Fork

NC 215

Brevard

French Broad

Headwaters Outfitters

West Fork

Rosman

US 64

← Cashiers

US 178

12 · COURTHOUSE CREEK ·

DIFFICULTY	IV/V
LENGTH	2 Miles
PUT-IN	Courthouse Falls
TAKE-OUT	US 215
ELEVATION	3425 to 2967 ft
GRADIENT	290,152
DRAINAGE	2.6 sq. mi.
GAUGE	Visual, French Broad @ Rosman, or 64 North Fork Bridge
LEVELS	3'+ on 64 Bridge or 2300+ at Rosman

BETA

paddler sam simmons - © LD

This little creek combines roadside ease of use, beautiful scenery, clean water, and the allure of a massive 40 footer upstream to tempt any paddler passing through the Balsams on a high water day. Runable when the North Fork French Broad gauge is over 3', this little stream provides some class IV fun for the intermediate running from the low water bridge down, or a huge ride for the serious waterfall addict who drives or ferries over and proceeds up the additional 1.5 miles to Courthouse Falls. Remember the rule of thumb—if the water is high enough to hit the door of your vehicle, don't drive through it. It would be a hell of a class V way to ruin your ride and your day—if you lived to tell the tale.

Below the low water bridge Courthouse Creek offers up some great class IV micro creeking, as long as you are wary of the potential for wood. Another gauge is located on the upsteam side of the 215 bridge at the bottom of the run, visible from your car when driving up the gravel road to the takout. Two feet is a good minimum level.

Shuttle: To reach the take out, drive 10.3 miles north from Rosman on NC 215. Head right on a forest service road just before 215 crosses the North Fork. Drive up this road 3 miles to the Courthouse Falls Trailhead and hike to the creek. If the water is high, an alternate lower put in can be used at the low water bridge. The take out is at the junction of the forest service road and 215.

13 · UPPER NORTH FORK FB ·

The Upper North Fork is a good option if you're pressed for time and the river is too high for the regular North Fork run and too low for Courthouse Creek. Although there is a somewhat steep class IV stretch in there, this run is mostly about running Bird Rock Falls—a clean 17 footer that is located in the Living Waters Tabernacle, which is clearly visible from the highway, and who diligently tries to keep everyone off of their property. As long as you keep a low profile you'll be fine—just head off the center of the 17 foot drop and keep on moving downstream. The rest of the run is largely flat, with one section of pretty good gradient and another waterfall which is usually portaged downstream of Bird Rock. If the water level is dropping while you're on the run, keep on going down through the regular run to Alligator Rock for a great longer creeking experience.

Shuttle: From the 64/215 junction near Rosman, head north on 215 about 6 miles to a left on state road 1326. Cross the river and park on the right for the take out. To reach the put in, continue north on 215 a little over 2.5 miles to a left turn across the river in Balsam Grove. Park here.

bird rock falls - paddler sam simmons - © LD

DIFFICULTY	IV
LENGTH	2.7 Miles
PUT-IN	Balsam Grove
TAKE-OUT	SR 1326
ELEVATION	2853 to 2618
GRADIENT	92,123,20
DRAINAGE	14.4 sq. mi.
GAUGE	US 64 NF Gauge or USGS FB @ Rosman
LEVELS	2'+ or 1000 cfs+

BETA

DIFFICULTY	IV (0' to 2') V (2'+)
LENGTH	2.9 miles
PUT-IN	Pullout on 215
TAKE-OUT	Aligator Rock
ELEVATION	2570 to 2278
GRADIENT	121, 129, 42
DRAINAGE	31.2 sq. mi.
GAUGE	USGS French Broad @ Rosman, or North Fork Bridge
LEVELS	minus 3" to 2.5' on Bridge or 350+ at Rosman

BETA

boxcar falls - paddler peter horne - © Rob Maxwell

the clog - paddlers matt walker and will lyons - ©LD

The North Fork of the French Broad has long been a super classic staple of WNC creeking, providing a highly scenic, super fun entry level adventure for aspiring hair boaters to cut their teeth on. The stream is small and has large, fun, pool/drop style rapids that allow paddlers to hone their skills while keeping the moves a step short of class V, and the beatings spectacular but survivable.

Slide into the large pool beneath the power lines at the put in, and head downstream through about 1/2 mile of warmup. The first horizon line is unmistakably huge, signifying the time to get out on river right and scout the largest drop—Boxcar Falls. Legend has it that in the early 1900s a boxcar fell from a small gauge logging railroad and was lost in the pool at the base of the falls. Don't let it happen to you! If the standard right line gets too easy after a few runs, give the "Blind Date" line on the left side

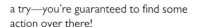
submarine - paddler phil foti - ©LD

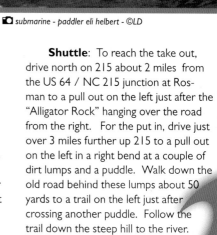
submarine - paddler eli helbert - ©LD

a try—you're guaranteed to find some action over there!

Below Boxcar, the gorge begins in earnest, with about a 1/2 dozen more good rapids. Be on the lookout for wood on either side of the island just downstream of Boxcar. After that the fun kicks in, with numerous slides and rapids including Razorback, the Clog, and Vortex, and culminating with Submarine—a blind horizon line which warrants a scout from river left. Be aware that the main hazard of this drop is the undercut wall that you're standing on when you scout. Below this, the river eases to class III for a mile or more, with beautiful scenery and fun little drops to keep you entertained. If you want to pass on the run out, look for

a picnic table in the woods on river left about 1/4 mile downstream of Submarine, and hike up the very steep trail from there to the road. Most people only try this option once. For another fun add-on if the river is above 1 foot, put in at the bridge at SR 1326 and run an extra 1.75 miles, including a fun upper slide known as "Sandpaper." When you reach the take-out, head back upstream before the water drops, because you're almost sure to want another run on this one!

Shuttle: To reach the take out, drive north on 215 about 2 miles from the US 64 / NC 215 junction at Rosman to a pull out on the left just after the "Alligator Rock" hanging over the road from the right. For the put in, drive just over 3 miles further up 215 to a pull out on the left in a right bend at a couple of dirt lumps and a puddle. Walk down the old road behind these lumps about 50 yards to a trail on the left just after crossing another puddle. Follow the trail down the steep hill to the river.

57

DIFFICULTY	IV/V
LENGTH	2.5 Miles
PUT-IN	SR 1309 Bridge
TAKE-OUT	Woodruff Rd.
ELEVATION	2534 to 2238
GRADIENT	121,129,41
DRAINAGE	18.8 sq. mi.
GAUGE	French Broad @ Rosman, or SR 1309 Br.
LEVELS	600+ cfs or -3" to 1.75' on the bridge

BETA

Put on your sliding shoes, this is going to be a fast one! This less paddled sister run of the classic North Fork is home to three big, fairly easy, super fun slides, and one long boulder garden rapid with a stompy hole at high water. The action begins about 1/4 mile below the put in with a slide into a vertical drop with a juicy hole. Scout left. The other two big drops are the next two rapids—each spaced 1/4 to 1/2 mile apart, with the biggest one coming last. Scout #2 on the left, and #3 from the right. After the final slide one large rapid remains. This rapid has a hole on the left at higher water that has been the site of several close calls, and which took the life of Western Carolina Paddlers founder Jim Sheppard. The safest bet is to hug the right bank through this boulder garden, especially at high water, as the tempting looking boof hump on river left often leads to a beating or worse. At the end of this rapid the river eases to class III then slowly to class II, then runs out some flatwater to highway 64. After passing under US 64, look for a break in the brush on the right 100-200 yards downstream that signifies the takeout.

Shuttle: From Headwaters Outfitters at the 64/215 junction, drive about 2.6 miles west on 64 to a right turn at a Citgo gas station on sr 1309. Follow this road about 2.2 miles to the put in at a bridge over the river. For the takeout, drive back down to 64 and head east, taking a right on Woodruff just before the bridge over the West Fork. Park in a pull out on the left about 100 yards up. Alternately, you can paddle on down to the Headwaters Outfitters at the confluence with the North Fork.

📷 *third drop - paddlers jah will and nik haase - ©LD*

Canton

Waynesville

US 276

East
Fork
Pigeon
River

Lake
Logan

Hwy. 215

Steel
Bridge
Gauge

Camp
Daniel
Boone

· FORKS
OF THE
PIGEON ·

West
Fork
Pigeon
River

Asheville

Sunburst

West
Fork

Little
East
Fork

Big
East
Fork
Trailhead

Big
East
Fork

Greasy Cove Prong

Middle
Prong

Culvert
Bridge

Garden
of the
Gods

Dark Prong

Brevard

Graveyard
Fields

Looking
Glass
Overlook

Upper
West
Fork

Flat Laurel

Blue Ridge Parkway

Rosman

16 · BIG EAST FORK ·

The Big East Fork of the Pigeon River is one of the finest stretches of whitewater in the Southeast, and is also possibly the hardest to catch with water and access. The steep gradient, clean water, and stunning scenery can largely be attributed to the fact that the put-in is right off the Blue Ridge Parkway in the Shining Rock Wilderness Area; unfortunately, the Parkway is closed for the bulk of the rainy season each year. That fact, combined with one of the smallest drainages in the area, makes the Big East Fork feel all the more magical when you finally put on. Look for heavy rains during periods of warm weather, usually April through November, and plan to be there within three hours of the end of the rain. The sure indicator is AFWS rain Gauge 1816, Daniel Ridge. If more than three inches has fallen in the last six hours, you should be good to go. Another good indication is a reading of 5 feet or more on the USGS West Fork Pigeon above Lake Logan Gauge.

From the Looking Glass Rock overlook at Parkway Mile Marker 417, walk down the Mountains to Sea Trail about a half mile to a small foot bridge over the river. If it looks like you won't need to push with your hands to get your boat over the rocks at the end of the pool under the bridge, you've got plenty of water. If you can't see rocks at the end of the pool, be prepared for some of the best and most intense class V+ creeking of your life!

The first half mile is steep and continuous, and usually pinny and low until the Dark Prong flows in from the left, doubling the flow and signaling the beginning of the goods. The next 1.5 miles hold some of the most unique whitewater in the country, with fairly frequent class

paddler trip kinney - photo kevin colburn

V drops that have a high elevation micro creeking feel that you won't get anywhere else in the East. Most of the drops on this creek are blind, and most have at least one route that will end in a pin, drop onto rocks, into wood, or land you in a nasty hole. Scouting is essential, but every drop on the Big East Fork is runable, and mishaps have been very few and far between.

Another large tributary entering from the left signals the end of the micro creeking and the beginning of the bigger drops. Get out on the right to scout or carry the first one, Triple Falls. Below Triple Falls the drops are increasingly separated by class III boogie water, until an eight foot drop into a narrow walled slot on river right signals the end of the hard stuff. The spacing of the rapids through this section allows for plenty of time to enjoy some of the best wilderness scenery in the state, but don't let down your guard; there are some complex drops in this section! The final drop, known as "Baby Gorilla," has dished out more spankings than any other drop on the run. Watch your elbows, wear a good helmet, and be ready to brace off the walls! After Baby Gorilla it's about 3/4 mile of class III/IV to the Highway 276 bridge and the takeout.

Note: Although the gradient on the map makes the mile above the put-in look enticing, you don't want to go there unless portaging around 100 footers through Rhododendron thickets is your idea of a good run.

Shuttle: To reach the take out, drive 2.9 miles north on US 276 from the Parkway to the Big East Fork Trailhead on river left, at the end of the long guard rail. For the put in, drive South on the Parkway from 276 to the Looking Glass Overlook at mile 417. Cross the road and hike 1/2 mile down the Mountains to Sea Trail to the foot bridge.

paddler tom visnius - photo kevin colburn

paddler leland - photo kevin colburn

DIFFICULTY	V
LENGTH	4.4 miles
PUT-IN	Looking Glass Overlook
TAKE-OUT	US 276
ELEVATION	4323 to 3353
GRADIENT	240, 330, 231, 125, 44
DRAINAGE	1.2 sq. mi.
GAUGE	Visual / AFWS Daniel Ridge
LEVELS	3" rain in past 6 hours on Daniel Ridge

BETA

17 · UPPER WEST FORK PIGEON ·

the big cascade - ©LD

BETA

DIFFICULTY	IV/V (V+)
LENGTH	1.4 miles
PUT-IN	above upper bridge
TAKE-OUT	upper bridge
ELEVATION	4812 to 4491
GRADIENT	244, 77
DRAINAGE	1.7 sq. mi.
GAUGE	USGS West Fork Pigeon Near Hazlewood/AFWS Mt. Hardy
LEVELS	3.5'+ at Hazlewood or 3+" Mt. Hardy

The Upper West Fork is a super high elevation run that you can jump on to get some entertainment when you rush to the highlands only to find everything else is just too high. This roadside run forms the border between the Shining Rock and Middle Prong Wilderness Areas—two of the most amazing protected wildernesses in the east.

Drop a shuttle car at the bridge above the Garden of the Gods and drive up the hill until you pass the big drop—a 60 foot 2 tiered cascade which is visible from the highway. Continue up the road about another mile, looking for a road which ducks through an opening in the brush on the left and down into a dirt parking lot. Park here and hope there's enough water to float your boat. Watch for wood.

Shuttle: The take out is at the first bridge on 215 above the culvert bridge. Put in as far upstream as the level looks boatable.

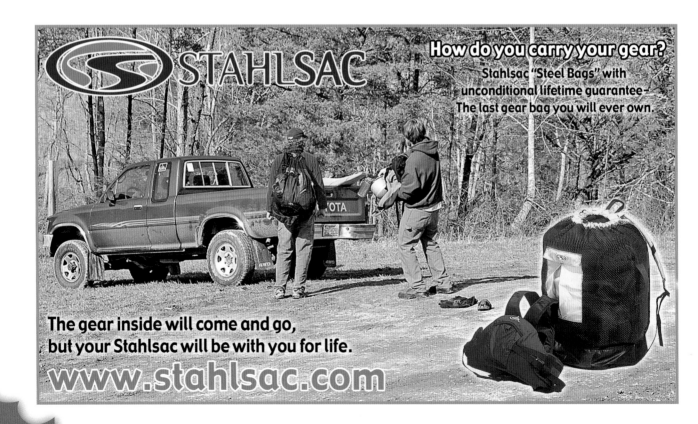

18 · GARDEN OF THE GODS ·

The unrepeated holy grail of southeastern hair boating flows defiantly in clear view of a well traveled reach of highway 215. Although the drop under the bridge and the one immediately above have seen a few super low water descents, and the stretch from the bridge down has been run by several parties, only one paddler has yet to link together the moves on the steepest half mile of runable looking whitewater in the East. Chip Collins ran this stretch about a dozen times more than a decade ago—in both hard boat and Thrillseeker—thinking that a couple of other boaters had done it before him. Those boaters have both said they never did, and nobody has run it since. Chip's comment was that when running that, "you're playing with your life." Every paddler will have to make their own assessment, but many of the best creekers in the world have driven on by the Garden's huge drops and hidden sieves to look for something a bit more in the reasonable class V+ range.

looking down the garden - ©LD

BETA	
DIFFICULTY	VI
LENGTH	1 mile
PUT-IN	Upper Bridge
TAKE-OUT	.3 miles below culvert bridge
ELEVATION	4485 to 3863
GRADIENT	622 (368 ft. in .4 miles)
DRAINAGE	5 sq. mi.
GAUGE	USGS West Fork Pigeon Near Retreat / Mt Hardy AFWS
LEVELS	2.5'?

If you're considering attempting a run here, you should hike the entire stretch before hand at a low level and a runable one, and you should have a good memory—'cause you're not going to be able to stop on the way down. Also, make sure you have a camera with you—so that we at least get a final photo with which we can remember you in edition II of this book.

Shuttle: From the put in for the regular West Fork run, drive south across the culvert bridge and continue to the next bridge. Take out by carrying 200 yards through the woods to the second grassy pullout on the right below the culvert bridge.

looking up the garden - ©LD

19 · WEST FORK PIGEON ·

If you're looking for an introduction to class V micro creeking that you can get to easily, look no further. The West Fork offers class IV/V creeking in a beautiful wilderness setting, while never wandering more than 1/2 mile from the highway. Furthermore, it runs after only moderately hard rainfall, has an internet gauge, and is 50 minutes from Asheville. The water quality is pristine, and the scenery is some of the finest to be found.

Walk down the wooded slope from the put in parking area about 200 yards to the river. At the point where you reach the river, there will be two islands that split the current into three channels. The floods of September, '04 diverted the water into the channel on the far side of both islands, so some wading will be required unless you walk to the downstream end of the islands to put in.

Boogie water will follow and will ease from class V- to class IV, then flatten into a short pool before becoming very bumpy scrapy class II/III. Don't despair, there are only two short sections of bone dogging, and the rest of the rapids are well worth it.

About half way into the run there are two items which warrant caution. The first is the largest rapid on the run, which occurs at the end of a bend to the right, with a rock slope coming down to the river on the left and a small stream cascading down the rocks (the second of two places that fit this description). Eddies are sparse at the top, so be alert. The top half of the rapid features a fast entrance to a narrow, curling slot into a big hole feeding under a boulder on the right. Scouting and carrying the top half of the rapid is easier on the right, but leaves no easy option for scouting or carrying the lower half. If you choose this option, aim for the center of the horizon line below—far left is to be avoided.

The second item of note is a river-wide old growth log which must be carried. It's located not far downstream of the rapid mentioned above, and it's blind with a fast approach, so be careful. Catch a last minute eddy on the left and get out, being aware that you are exiting your boat on top of some small sieves. Just below this are two more rapids which warrant some scouting. Below this, the last item of note is a 10 foot falls. The final mile is a class II-IV boogie water runout to the car.

Shuttle: Take 215 south 2.9 miles from the bridge at the head of Lake Logan to Sunburst Rec Area. Pass the rec area, cross the bridge over the Middle Prong, and park on the left at the take out. To reach the put in, continue up 215 to the culvert bridge over the Garden of the Gods. Backtrack about .3 miles on 215 to the second grassy pullout on the right. Hike 250 yards through the woods to reach the creek.

DIFFICULTY	V
LENGTH	3.8 miles
PUT-IN	.3 miles below culvert bridge
TAKE-OUT	Sunburst Rec Area
ELEVATION	3863 to 3152
GRADIENT	247, 207, 177, 80
DRAINAGE	7.4 sq. mi.
GAUGE	USGS W.Fk Pigeon Near Hazlewood/AFWS Mt. Hardy
LEVELS	2.5' to 3.5' at Hazlewood

BETA

paddler andria baldovin - ©LD

20 · MIDDLE PRONG ·

DIFFICULTY	V
LENGTH	2 miles
PUT-IN	hike in
TAKE-OUT	Sunburst Rec Area
ELEVATION	3792 to 3134
GRADIENT	421, 237
DRAINAGE	6.6 sq. mi.
GAUGE	USGS W.Fk Pigeon Near Hazlewood/AFWS Mt. Hardy
LEVELS	3'+ at Hazlewood

BETA

paddler bill alexander - photo dawn powell

This cryptic little cousin of the West Fork drains possibly the prettiest wilderness in the southeast, and is as hard to catch with water as it is beautiful. Turn off of 215 onto the road just after the Sunburst Rec Area and before the bridge over the Middle Prong, and drive up over the low water bridge through the right hand prong, parking in the gravel lot just beyond on the left. Put your boat on your shoulder and start walking up the road. When the road switches hard back to the right, you can either stay on the road to access the super steeps at the top, or continue on the trail for a short distance and then drop down along a small tributary to do only the more commonly run lower mile.

If you choose the upper mile, continue on until the road turns to trail and drops to the creek—looking carefully for the huge waterfall that bears serious examination at the top. The large drop has never been run, the rapid right below it is usually a walk, and the mile downstream of them is not for the faint of heart.

The lower mile is not to be taken lightly, either. There is at least one rapid that is portaged more than it is run, several other good sized drops, and the river is always choked with some serious wood at one place or another. Just the sight of the complicated rapid right at the put-in is enough to make some paddlers start the run with a walk. While the hike, wood, and difficulty of catching this run with water will keep you from running

this creek many times—it's certainly well worth exploring this little stream if only to check off another adventure in a stunningly beautiful place.

Shuttle: Take 215 south 2.9 miles from the bridge at the head of Lake Logan to Sunburst Rec Area. Just past the rec area, turn right on a gravel road before the bridge over the Middle Prong. Continue on this road until you drive through a creek, then park in the gravel lot on the left just before the gate. Carry upstream on the gravel road through one switchback, then stay straight on a smaller path (old roadbed) when the road turns up the mountain again. Continue on the path until it ends at a small stream. Follow the stream down to the river.

paddler dawn powell - photo bill alexander

21 · THE BATHTUBS ·

paddler ryan bednar - photo brit farthing

DIFFICULTY	V-
LENGTH	2 miles
PUT-IN	Hike
TAKE-OUT	Camp Daniel Boone
ELEVATION	4261 to 3293
GRADIENT	580, 304
DRAINAGE	1.8 sq. mi.
GAUGE	visual - low water bridge
LEVELS	2" over the bridge is minimum

BETA

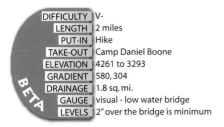

The Bathtubs section of the Little East Fork is almost never done, but has a high enough fun factor that it certainly warrants a mention. Running from the heart of the Shining Rock Wilderness to the base of Cold Mountain, this little stream is an anomaly among Balsam area creeks, with the lower mile offering some excellent steep continuous boulder garden style rapids more reminiscent of a run you would find in the Smokies. For those willing to make the hike to the steep upper mile, they will be rewarded with the mythical clean bedrock style drops and slides of the Bathtubs, which few boaters have ever seen.

This run is not accessible all the time since you must drive through the Daniel Boone Boy Scout Camp to reach the takeout—and other than knowing that summer is a no-go, there is no good way to determine if a group will be using the camp at any given time. When no groups are there, the folks at the camp are friendly as long as you are respectful of camp property, drive slowly, and park well out of traffic on the road above the camp. Cross the low water bridge on foot and hike up the obvious trail on river left.

Shuttle: From Canton, take NC 110 to the NC 215/US 276 junction. From Waynesville, take US 276 to the NC 215/US 276 junction. Take 215 south, staying on 215 by taking a left turn at the T-junction near Retreat. From the T, continue just over 2 miles to a left on Little East Fork Rd. Follow Little East Fork Rd. for several miles, passing through Camp Daniel Boone, and pull out on the right just before the gated bridge over the river. Walk across the bridge and hike up river left to the put in.

paddler max keller - photo brit farthing

paddler nik haase - photo brit farthing

SOUTHERN ESCARPMENT

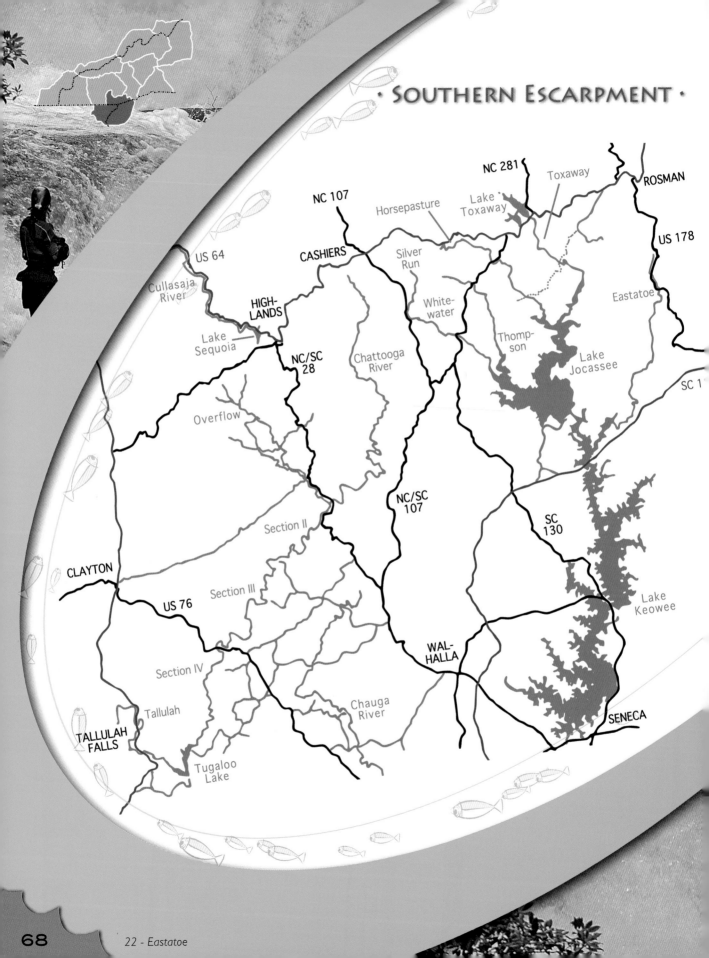

NC 281

Toxaway

ROSMAN

NC 107

Horsepasture

Lake Toxaway

US 178

US 64

CASHIERS

Silver Run

Eastatoe

Cullasaja River

HIGH-LANDS

White-water

Thompson

Lake Jocassee

Lake Sequoia

NC/SC 28

Chattooga River

SC 1

Overflow

NC/SC 107

SC 130

Section II

CLAYTON

Section III

SC 130

Lake Keowee

US 76

WAL-HALLA

Section IV

Tallulah

Chauga River

TALLULAH FALLS

SENECA

Tugaloo Lake

22 · EASTATOE ·

DIFFICULTY	IV+
LENGTH	3.7 miles
PUT-IN	US 178
TAKE-OUT	Second Bridge
ELEVATION	1650 to 961
GRADIENT	186,228,215,60
DRAINAGE	6.5 sq. mi.
GAUGE	visual
LEVELS	

BETA

📷 *rapid below the portage - paddler will reeves - photo brad roberts*

📷 *first falls - paddler shayne day - photo brad roberts*
📷 *upper corner: the portage - photo brad roberts*

If you're into log jams, bumpy slides, and epic portages, you've just found the perfect run. Eastatoe Creek flows from the NC/SC state line steeply down the Southern Escarpment through a super rugged gorge and into Lake Keowee. From the moment it leaves the houses and dirt roads surrounding the putin, it drops through a boxed in rhododendron jungle and over large drops that are often filled with logs. The first drop—a fairly easy slide—is blind, so be on the lookout for the horizon line and grab an eddy to check for wood. This will be the overwhelming theme of any day on Eastatoe—grab an eddy, check for wood.

There will be about a half dozen decent sized drops or slides in the first 1.75 miles, leading up to the portage. Although lots of folks seem to think the portage would be easier on the left, I haven't heard of a single person actually doing it that way, and it's certainly going to be easier to scout the drop just below the portage from river right. Make sure you have a good rope to lower yourself and your boat off a tree, and wear long pants in summer to protect against the copious stinging nettles and poison ivy. The drop below the portage is probably the most fun on the run as long as a little spine compression doesn't bother you.

The main things to keep in mind when attempting this run are that it requires an absolutely huge rain, and the take-out is going to be tricky on the trespassing/private property end. Please be respectful with where and how you park, and try to keep a low profile in the communities on both ends of the run. Park along 178 at the put in, and along the public road at the takeout, although this will require paddling some flatwater through the farmlands at the end of the run.

Shuttle: From highway 64 near Rosman, take US 178 South 9 miles to the put-in bridge over the Eastatoe. To reach the take out, continue 4.9 miles south on 178 to a right turn on old highway 11. Follow this road to the bridge over the creek.

· JOCASSEE DRAINAGE ·

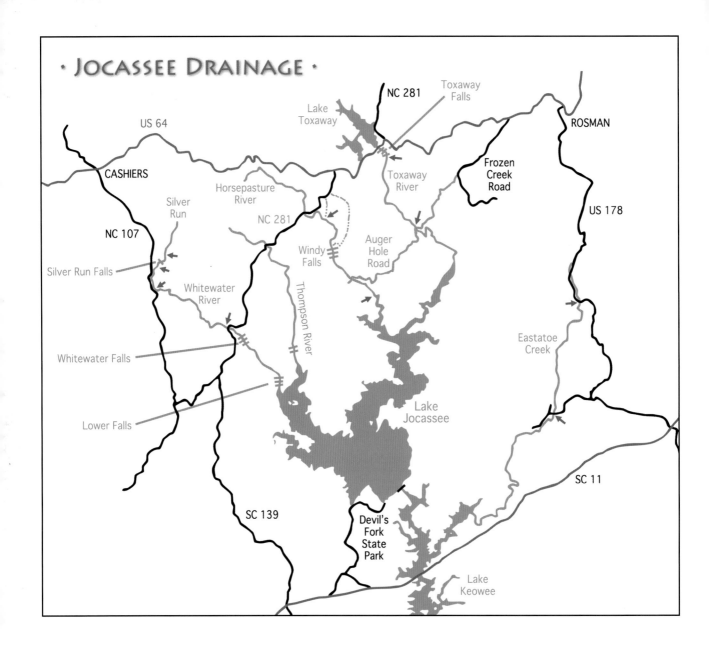

Lake Toxaway

Toxaway Falls

NC 281

ROSMAN

US 64

CASHIERS

Horsepasture River

Toxaway River

Frozen Creek Road

US 178

Silver Run

NC 281

NC 107

Windy Falls

Auger Hole Road

Silver Run Falls

Whitewater River

Thompson River

Whitewater Falls

Eastatoe Creek

Lower Falls

Lake Jocassee

SC 139

SC 11

Devil's Fork State Park

Lake Keowee

If there really is an edge of the World, it's located in the Jocassee drainage. The 4 runs listed here have an average overall gradient of 297 feet per mile, with some of the finest granite and largest runable drops and slides anywhere. Yes, including California. These runs are tremendously committing, with rugged and often inescapable gorges, difficult and dangerous portages, and rapids so large that you're certain to be somewhat shell shocked after a first trip on any of them. Jocassee is also home to two other lesser known creeks. The Thompson, which also sports some 500+ foot miles of whitewater and has only seen a handfull of runs to this date, and Toxaway Creek—a flatwater and portage fest that is to be avoided at all cost—no matter how good it looks on the topo. No matter which of the Jocassee runs you're tackling, bring lots of ropes, rescue gear, food, a breakdown, flashlight, and your largest set of cahones—you're gonna need them all in here.

a whitewater fairy tale at stairstep falls, horsepasture river - paddler ben hayes - © LD

23 · TOXAWAY ·

If you're into gigantic, high speed, hair raising, bedrock granite slides and sluices, but don't have the time or inclination to head to California, don't despair; there's a little piece of California tucked away in an appalachian state park where the smog isn't so thick and the price of gas is a lot lower. The Toxaway is a classic California style run, complete with enormous slides, epic portages, tricky shuttle details, and a brutal carry out at the end—the only thing missing is a paddle across a lake. Nevertheless, the Toxaway offers by far the largest slides in the eastern US, and is a must do for serious gradient aficionados.

Access is very sensitive here, and leaving a car in the wrong place is a great way to screw it up for everyone. It's also a good way to attract the attention of the police and Gorges Park Rangers and have your car towed. While access is still open at this time, there has been talk of the park no longer allowing kayaking. All groups should contact Park Superintendent Steve S. Pagano at 828-966-9099 before heading to do the run. Park on the north side of highway 64, in an out-of-the-way spot near the small business just east of the bridge over the top of Toxaway Falls. Cross the road and walk a bit farther east to a break in the guard rail, heading down the old road and angling down the ridge to the base of the falls.

DIFFICULTY	V+
LENGTH	3.7
PUT-IN	Toxaway Falls
TAKE-OUT	Auger Hole Road
ELEVATION	2698 to 1438
GRADIENT	291, 596, 245, 128
DRAINAGE	8 sq. mi.
GAUGE	Upstream river right at top of falls
LEVELS	no higher than 0

paddler dinver mcclure - © LD

paddler dinver mcclure - © LD

The river starts out fairly mellow until it meanders through the woods in braided channels around some islands. Get out and scout, because the first rapid of consequence is a 15 foot drop just beyond the island. Below here you will need to be on your toes - scouting often as the gradient slowly builds to a fever pitch over the next 1.75 miles. Several drops must be portaged, and although there are routes on river right for those who know them, the easiest option for those who don't know their way is usually to portage river left. When you reach a 100 foot tall monster of a drop that starts with a very steep 30 foot chute before spreading out onto a gigantic bumpy slide, you'll know the worst is over. This is Wintergreen Falls—and despite the rumors that it can't be portaged, there is a fairly easy scramble down a gully on river right if your hair has been raised enough for the day.

Below Wintergreen there are several more decent smaller rapids as well as plenty of wood to look out for in the river bed as you paddle the final 1.5 miles to the bridge at Auger Hole Road. Hopefully you've saved some energy - walk to the left 3.25 miles and 1000 vertical feet to your takeout car on Frozen Creek Road, and hope the beer you left in there is still nice and cold. Make sure that you're out before the park closes at dark lest you draw the attention of the rangers and get ticketed and/or locked in.

Shuttle: To reach the git in, take US 64 to the bridge over the top of Toxaway Falls. Park just east of the bridge near the small business located in an old quarry. To reach the git out, head east on 64 6.2 miles to Frozen Creek Road on the right. Take Frozen Creek Road 2.8 miles to the Gorges State Park lot.

paddler dinver mcclure - © LD

paddler dinver mcclure - ©LD

thrasher pike ramp b - paddler jonathan shanin - ©LD

DIFFICULTY	V+
LENGTH	3.7 miles
PUT-IN	Rainbow Falls
TAKE-OUT	Lake Jocassee
ELEVATION	2662 to 1186
GRADIENT	366, 911, 200, 9
DRAINAGE	25 sq. mi.
GAUGE	Visual / www.cashiers-nc.com
LEVELS	1" + rain, Cullasaja 4.5'+, FB Rosman 600+

BETA

first descent 2 drops above windy - paddler chris harjes - ©LD

This ultra classic bedrock shelf style run is a must do for serious creekers who want to experience the best of what the Jocassee drainage has to offer. The 1.5 miles of river which comprise the heart of the run between Rainbow Falls and Windy Falls averages well over 400 feet per mile with all drops runable. Take your camera, because the huge clean rapids of this river are some of the most photogenic in the East.

WARNING: Do not attempt to access the river upstream at the 281 bridge—all of the property is private, and attempted access will result in you being surrounded by angry blunt object wielding miners until the sheriff arrives to write you a very expensive ticket for trespassing.

From the Gorges parking lot, walk back to 281 and left down the highway a short distance to a gated road heading into the woods. Follow this road as it turns to trail and drops 3/4 mile down to the river at Turtleback Falls. After running Turtleback, waste no time getting out to walk Rainbow Falls as eddies get scarce near the edge, and tourists wash to their deaths over the falls every summer. Carry down the obvious river left trail and put back in from the spray soaked boulders near the base of the falls. The first half mile below the falls contains many complicated boulder rapids, punctuated by one 12 foot ledge with a shallow landing. You'll know the pace is about to pick up when you reach the horizon line at Stairstep Falls—a multi-tiered 70 foot tall cascade straight

out of a whitewater fairy tale. A variety of lines are possible, with a good trail on the left for scouting. If you're at all apprehensive about continuing downstream, this is the time to hike out, as the trail essentially ends here.

Below Stairstep the rapids pick up in size and difficulty, passing through a Raven's Fork style rapid, the two massive drops of Sidepocket Falls (A.K.A. Thrasher Pike), a super fast and very long two stage low angle slide known as Highway to Heaven, and several other large shelf style drops. The last rapid before leaving the river is a nasty 2 stage drop with a hole between stages that feeds left into a disgusting log/sieve combo that can be run or portaged right. Look for

paddler chris harjes - ©LD

highway to heaven - paddler amos shuman - ©LD

a small cliff wall on river left below here that signals time to get out (below the cliff wall). You will want to pass your boats up through a notch, then follow the trail downstream to a campsite at the top of Windy Falls. There are two huge runable drops near the campsite if you have the time and energy for more rapids.

Regroup, fuel up, and hydrate here, because now it's time to pay your dues. There are two options for exit from the gorge—a 1 mile portage around Windy Falls and a paddle out to the lake, or a 4.5 mile walk back to the Gorges State Park lot where your journey began. Either way, hike the obvious trail up the steep hill from the campsite. If you're portaging the falls, hike about 1/4 - 1/2 mile on this trail

until you see a fairly wide ridge sloping off to your right when the trail makes a flat curve to the left. Hike down this ridge almost a mile through the woods to the river, bearing right of some large rocks and following an old logging road to the river. Put back in for the final 1.5 miles of high quality class III+ to the lake. From here it's 7.75 miles of lake to the boat ramp at Devil's Fork State Park. You can hire a boat from Hoyett's (www.hoyetts. com - 864-944-9016) to shuttle you this distance, but make sure you arrive at the rendez-vous point on time. If you're spontaneous, cheap, late, or training for a California multi-day and need to hike out, continue up the trail until it merges with a road, and follow the road back to the parking area, making sure that you're out

before the lot closes at dark. As long as it's not a Sunday, you can avoid this issue by poaching some parking in the massive lot of the Baptist Church at Sapphire a short distance north on 281. If the church is having a bar-b-que, I highly recommend stopping in for some excellent post-river grub as well.

Shuttle: To reach the put in, take US 64 to NC 281 South between Rosman and Cashiers. Go south on 281 about 1 mile to the Gorges State Park lot entrance on the left. To reach the git out, continue down 281 (which turns to SC 130 at the state line) to SC 11. Go left (east) on SC 11 1.5 miles to a left turn. Follow the signs to Devil's Fork State Park.

24.2 · HORSIN' AROUND ·

📷 *windy falls bivy - paddler lee belknap - photo victor jones*

It was a 30 degree, mid December weekend in 1986, and we weren't sure which day we would finish. Victor Jones had been waiting a long time to make the first decent of the Horsepasture. Since this first decent was his idea, I happily volunteered to do the second right behind him. A year or so later, the Horsepasture would become the shortest and tallest river in the Wild and Scenic river system. We had done much hiking and scouting leading up to the trip and we camped at the put in so we could get an early start with our modern camping gear laden creek boats (Dancers!).

We landed like skipping stones at the bottom of "Bust Yer Butt Falls", slid over Turtleback falls, and walked, slid, and fell around the portage for the 100 foot high Rainbow Falls. The tiny drops we'd seen from the top of Rainbow turned out to be ten footers, and we creeked our way down to the next falls, and then the next, and then the next, running or portaging as needed. One of those falls was the hundred foot or so Staircase falls, with every one of its high shallow ledges runable that day.

As the day became late, we reached the part of the river we hadn't pre-scouted. We knew we had one more waterfall to go, but we knew nothing about it. Not even enough to be worried. We arrived at a typical boulder jumble, and Victor disappeared into a blind eddy above a large drop. As I started to join him, he suddenly appeared and motioned to stop. He was trapped above the last falls and was unable to exit his boat without shore based assistance.

We scouted and saw the easy portage. We congratulated ourselves for finishing the run in only a day. We were done! We had succeeded! We were elated. During the portage we rounded a boulder and could see downstream. It was the most ominous horizon line I have ever seen! We were in trouble! This was the top of what we later learned was Windy Falls—a 700 ft. series of waterfalls.

We portaged. We scrambled, we clung, clawed and roped. We swung between trees and handed our boats across. After roping down one very large steep rock face, we found ourselves boxed in by cliffs on each side with waterfalls above and below. To escape we rappelled exactly half the length of my 75 ft throw rope. The sun set.

As darkness set in, I knew exactly what to look for on those impossibly steep slopes. I found where a large, ancient tree had once fallen. The root ball had created a hollow bench that was barely big enough for boats, sleeping quarters, and a small fire. The full moon rose late, and we were as isolated as anyone in the eastern US can be. Our booties froze early, and we used the moonlight to find firewood. We didn't have nearly enough camping gear, yet it seemed like a nearly perfect adventure!

We rigged up an adequate sleeping pad and covers, and sat up late, dozing off around the small fire. While dozing, I'd have the strangest dreams of kayaking off of tall waterfalls and spiraling down past incredibly beautiful cliffs. I would always wake up before hitting the bottom or falling into the fire.

The next morning was uneventful. We immediately found the end of what would have been a far easier portage trail. After portaging a few more "smaller" falls the river leveled out and at mid morning we ran into some fishermen parked at the Auger Hole Road. If only we had found this during our pre-scouting expeditions. It took the rest of the day to reach the other end of the windy Lake Jocassee. Sometime around dark, with shuttle complete, Victor phoned home just in time to prevent a call to the rescue squad.

Lee Belknap

25 · SILVER RUN FALLS ·

DIFFICULTY	V+
LENGTH	.15 miles
PUT-IN	Silver Run Falls Parking Area
TAKE-OUT	Same
ELEVATION	3381 to 3276
GRADIENT	105
DRAINAGE	2.4 sq. mi.
GAUGE	Visual
LEVELS	

BETA

This fast twisty slide into a vertical 30 footer is an excellent if very difficult park & huck drop with which you can open a trip to the Whitewater. Park in the Silver Run Falls parking area and follow the obvious signs to the falls. Although you might be tempted to paddle down to the normal Whitewater run from here, don't—several excellent boaters have had near misses in a sieved out slide downstream of here. It's better to take out and drive downstream to the normal Whitewater put in.

Shuttle: Take NC 107 south from Cashiers 4 miles to the Silver Run Falls parking area.

📷 ©LD

26 · UPPER WHITEWATER ·

The Whitewater is the easiest run in the Jocassee drainage in terms of logistics and time required, but don't let this fool you—it's still a stout run with several huge class V+ rapids. Unlike the other Jocassee streams, the Whitewater is crossed by a highway before the gradient gets out of hand, removing the need for epic portages or lengthy hikes out. It is one of the most beautiful runs on the planet, but the same rhododendrons, doghobble, and thorn vines that keep it so unspoiled also make scouting and portaging a bitch. Wear long pants if the weather will allow.

The Whitewater has long spaces between the major rapids, allowing boaters to challenge some large drops without the relentless pressure of some of the other Jocassee runs. The trade off, however, is that the sections between large rapids tend to be quite bumpy, even at levels where the larger drops get juicy. The rocks are also sharper than the other Jocassee runs, leading to some serious boat abuse in the best of circumstances on this chewy little creek.

Find a wide spot between the highway and the river and pull out. Gear up, then drop down the bank and into the stream for 1/2 mile of thrashing through the rhododendrons, thorns, and strainers that litter the flat streambed. Another mile of class II follows as you work your way down towards the gorge. The first horizon line is a terminal unrunnable sieve—and the eddy at the lip is guarded by a fairly decent directional wave at higher levels. Portage right. About 80 yards downstream of here there is a beast of a vertical walled canyon that starts with a totally innocent looking slide. Make sure you get out above this—although the canyon has seen two runs, it is usually choked with wood, is often less than a boat length wide and is inescapable once you run the slide. Most people portage high on a trail through the woods on the left, although it is possible to seal launch in and run the 25 footer at the exit of the mini-gorge if you portage right.

Below here, the river has some large drops, most of which are easy to recognize and scout. The largest drop is 55 mph, a fast right curving slide into a 12 foot vertical drop with a nasty piton rock hidden in the landing that has many years of history destroying kayaks. The landing has undercuts and often wood just behind it, so scout carefully before running the drop. Several more large rapids will bring you to the final drop, a 20 foot vertical drop run on the right. The landing on this one is quite shallow—about 4 feet deep. If your spine is feeling too long you can boof on the right side, or you can portage left and save your back for another day.

Just out of site of the takeout bridge there is a 5' ledge drop that develops a terminal hole on river left at high water. Scout or portage right.

Shuttle: To reach the take out, drive south on 281 from the Sapphire/Toxaway area 7.8 miles to the bridge over the Whitewater. Pull out just before the bridge on the right. To reach the put in, continue down 281 another 1.9 miles and make a right on the connector which goes to highway 107. When you reach 107, make a right and go north just over 4 miles and find a pullout when you see the river on the right.

📷 *55 mph - © LD*

DIFFICULTY	V/V+
LENGTH	3.9 miles
PUT-IN	hwy 107
TAKE-OUT	hwy 281
ELEVATION	3236 to 2679
GRADIENT	44, 140, 211, 162
DRAINAGE	4.9 sq. mi.
GAUGE	281 Bridge
LEVELS	0 - 1.5'

BETA

📷 *falls exiting the mini-gorge - whitewater river - © LD*

📷 *keith sprinkle - whitewater river - © LD*

CHATTOOGA AREA

· CHATTOOGA AREA ·

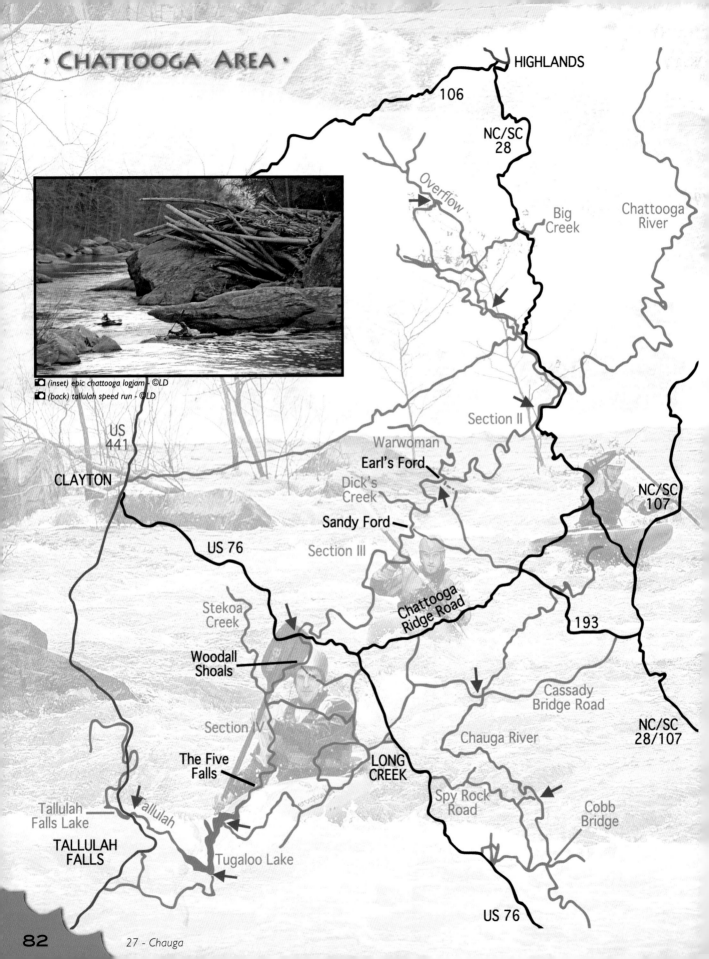

(inset) epic chattooga logjam - ©LD

(back) tallulah speed run - ©LD

HIGHLANDS

106

NC/SC
28

Overflow

Big
Creek

Chattooga
River

Section II

Warwoman

Earl's Ford

Dick's
Creek

Sandy Ford

Section III

NC/SC
107

US
441

CLAYTON

US 76

Chattooga
Ridge Road

193

Stekoa
Creek

Woodall
Shoals

Cassady
Bridge Road

Chauga River

NC/SC
28/107

Section IV

LONG
CREEK

The Five
Falls

Spy Rock
Road

Cobb
Bridge

Tallulah
Falls Lake

Tallulah

TALLULAH
FALLS

Tugaloo Lake

US 76

27 · CHAUGA ·

BETA	
DIFFICULTY	IV
LENGTH	6.75 miles
PUT-IN	Cassidy Bridge
TAKE-OUT	FR 1109
ELEVATION	1230 to 883
GRADIENT	28,66,100,64,68,18,3
DRAINAGE	37.2 sq. mi.
GAUGE	Cassidy Bridge Gauge
LEVELS	0 - 1.5'

paddler steve besch - john pruitt photo

The Chauga River is a fun class IV creek which parallels the Chattooga, dumping into Lake Hartwell near Westminster, SC. If you're in the Chattooga area and the river surges to a level at which you don't want to try Section IV, the Chauga makes a great alternate, with the put in and take out each about 20 minutes from the 76 Chattooga bridge. Keep in mind, however, that the Chattooga and Chauga drain from totally different areas—so high water on the Chattooga is not a sure indication that the Chauga is running. If you've just spent a rainy night in Long Creek, though, odds are pretty good.

After putting in under the Cassidy Bridge, a small slide rapid will be found shortly downstream. Next up will be the largest drop—Super Soc-Em-Dog. Scout or portage Super Soc-Em-Dog on the left, or aim for one of the launching pads on the right and air it out over the hole. Below this the Chauga enters a steep pine filled gorge, and winds its way through several more fun drops as it heads for the flatlands of the upstate. At lower water you will want to take out at the normal takeout, but at higher flows (>6") you can continue down another 2.25 miles to Cobbs Bridge, running 12 foot Riley Moore Falls which breaks up the flat water along the way. Which ever you choose, you're sure to remember a day spent on this unique low elevation pine forest creek run, and you'll be back for more the next time you get "rained out" on Section IV.

Shuttle: From the 76 bridge over the Chattooga, head east 6.5 miles to where Spy Rock Road cuts off to the left in a bend to the right. Take Spy Rock Road 3.7 miles, bearing right at the major fork 1.4 miles in. Turn left on FR 1109, and follow it to the wide area at the end. If you have high clearance or 4x4, you can proceed down the steep road to the river. For the alternate take out, continue on Spy Rock Road to the T junction, and head left to the first bridge. To reach the put in, return to 76 and head west 2 miles to Longcreek. Make a right on Academy Road at the Bucket T Restaurant. Go 1.5 miles to a right on Cassidy Bridge Road, and follow Cassidy Bridge to a left turn just before the bridge. Pull off and park near the river.

super soc-em-dog - paddler carter fay - © rob maxwell

· FORBIDDEN FRUIT ·

· THE REST OF A SOUTHEASTERN CLASSIC ·

You probably know virtually nothing about the headwaters of the Chattooga River. This is because it is illegal to paddle this beautiful 21 mile section of river, and has been for nearly thirty years. How is this possible you ask, given that the river is on public land and was designated as both Wilderness and as Wild and Scenic specifically for boaters and other non motorized users to enjoy? American Whitewater has been asking the same question since 1995 and we finally got an answer in 2004.

Boating was originally banned to grant a small group of well connected anglers a

boater-free river. We pushed hard for the Forest Service to review the policy, and in 2004 the Sumter National Forest decided almost unbelievably to uphold the boating ban. They made this decision based on a value-laden look at the issues which had no data, no studies, no legal arguments, and no rational arguments to support it. They claimed that paddling and angling were incompatible uses of the river, and that paddlers could and should simply go elsewhere. Paddlers were portrayed as second class citizens that are incapable of appreciating Wilderness and that ruin others' Wilderness experiences.

The Decision flies in the face of virtually every law governing the Forest Service and any concept of equality. It would spell disaster for river recreation Nationwide if it is accepted by the Forest Service that paddlers do not belong in Wilderness or on Wild and Scenic Rivers, and that we should be zoned away from other recreationists. American Whitewater has formally appealed this flawed decision and we will not stop until we can all legally paddle the Headwaters of the Chattooga, and until our public rivers are managed fairly.

all photos ©LD

American Whitewater is the voice of whitewater rivers and of the community of paddlers that cherish those rivers. We work every day to make sure that these rivers are not monopolized by dam owners, gutted by timber and mining companies, sold into development, or otherwise mismanaged. We counter the constant pressure to profit from rivers at the public's expense, and help empower paddlers to be strong and effective river stewards. If it were not for the work of the American Whitewater community, our rivers would suffer, and decision makers would rarely even consider

whitewater recreation. We hope that the readers of this book will join American Whitewater and become part of the community of paddlers working to protect and restore the spectacular rivers of the Southern Appalachians. Get involved at www.americanwhitewater.org.

Kevin Colburn

Section 00

Section Double Zero of the Chattooga is the most difficult section of the entire river, ranking as a class V creek run with the usual array of wood, sieves, potholes, and big drops. This very small creek transports paddlers over 5 to 8 foot tall sliding ledges while forcing them to duck through laurel thickets and under bogus no trespassing signs. Paddlers soon arrive at the lip of a 20 foot sketchy drop, followed by unique series of rapids and falls. One rapid courses through a narrow gorge with smooth vertical walls. This memorable rapid opens up just in time for paddlers to catch a small eddy above a nasty sieve, which can then be walked. After the sieve, there are some small challenging drops followed by long shallow bedrock slides with shallow holes. The river then mellows until the last two rapids above the takeout which are Class IV or V.

DIFFICULTY	V
LENGTH	5.25 miles
PUT-IN	Bull Pen Bridge
TAKE-OUT	Burrell's Ford
ELEVATION	2415 to 2047
GRADIENT	147,112,44,20,26,19
DRAINAGE	
GAUGE	
LEVELS	

Section 0

Section 0 is a pristine, beautiful creek run that allows paddlers the chance to paddle through the federally designated Ellicott Rock Wilderness. Distinct Class III and IV rapids and ledges begin shortly after rounding the first bend and continue until Super Corkscrew is reached. Super Corkscrew is a technical Class V rapid that can be scouted and portaged on river right. Next is about another mile of class III and IV boulder gardens followed by a mile or two of class II. Section 0 requires less water than the Section 00 and was a favorite of paddlers prior to the ban because of its scenic beauty, high quality rapids, and relatively little flatwater.

DIFFICULTY	III/IV (V)
LENGTH	5.25 miles
PUT-IN	Grimshawes Bridge
TAKE-OUT	Bull Pen Bridge
ELEVATION	2786 to 2415
GRADIENT	87,105,39,47,61,32
DRAINAGE	
GAUGE	
LEVELS	

Section 1

Section One of the Chattooga is the longest of the headwaters sections, characterized by relatively large distinct rapids and drops separated by stretches of scenic flatwater. The first significant rapid is Class V+ Big Bend Falls, which is followed by numerous other Class IV and V drops, including the Rock Gorge. After the Rock Gorge the river (yes, it is now a full fledged river), flattens out for several miles to the take out.

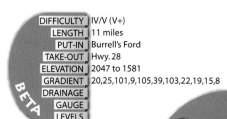

DIFFICULTY	IV/V (V+)
LENGTH	11 miles
PUT-IN	Burrell's Ford
TAKE-OUT	Hwy. 28
ELEVATION	2047 to 1581
GRADIENT	20,25,101,9,105,39,103,22,19,15,8
DRAINAGE	
GAUGE	
LEVELS	

28 · Overflow ·

Singley's Falls - © Rob Maxwell

© Rob Maxwell

Milt Aitken runs "Gravity"

This super classic Chattooga tributary boasts incredible scenery, excellent but manageable class V drops, and one of the richest histories of any southeastern creek. Alan Singley did the first two runs of this creek solo in the mid seventies, and the run grew to be a popular if hard to catch creeking staple in the eighties. 30 years after is was explored, Overflow remains as one of the best runs in the south—with a difficulty very comparable to the Narrows of the Green with the exception of Gorilla and Sunshine.

Below the put in, the creek winds through some easier drops and slides for a while before gorging up and dropping over the larger drops of Blind Falls and Gravity—both of which can be scouted from the right. From here, there are several more good class V drops before the confluence with Holcombe and Big Creeks at Three Forks, including the largest drop—Singley's Falls, which is somewhat blind (like most Overflow rapids) and should be scouted on the left. After the confluence, the creek drops over the two most formidable rapids—The Great Marginal Monster and Pinball—before mellowing into the runout to the bridge at the end. Almost every Overflow rapid harbors a pothole or cave or other feature to be avoided, so scouting is recommended—it's also a great way to stop and enjoy the scenery of this amazing creek.

Shuttle: From the highway 28 bridge over the Chattooga, go north 2.25 miles to a left turn signed to Clayton. Drive .2 miles and make a right before the bridge over the West Fork on Overflow Creek Road. Follow this road and park just across the first bridge for the takeout. To reach the put in, continue up Overflow Creek Road for several miles, parking where the road crosses the creek again. Note that the road will cross Holcomb Creek first—don't make the mistake of putting in on this unrunable stream.

DIFFICULTY	V
LENGTH	6.4 miles
PUT-IN	Billingsley Creek Road
TAKE-OUT	Overflow Creek Road Bridge
ELEVATION	2463 to 1675
GRADIENT	81, 199, 86, 132, 234, 45, 11
DRAINAGE	4.8 sq. mi.
GAUGE	Overflow Creek Road Bridge
LEVELS	.7' to 2'

BETA

Section II of the Chattooga is a scenic class II float through southern pine forest, sprinkled with occasional shoals and rapids, and having one larger class III- rapid towards the end. Along with beginning kayakers, this run is a favorite of tubers and canoe campers, providing a great outing in a warm wilderness easily accessible from the Upstate and Atlanta. Put in at the parking area off of highway 28 and paddle 5.7 miles to the beach at Earl's Ford on river left—across from where Warwoman Creek flows in.

Shuttle: From the US 76 Chattooga bridge, drive east 2 miles to Chattooga Ridge Road on the left. Take Chattooga Ridge Road 5.85 miles to Earl's Ford Road, and go left. Drop your take out car at the end of this road in the Earl's Ford parking lot. To reach the put in, return to Chattooga Ridge Road and go left, continuing until you run into highway 28. Go left on 28 a little over 4 miles to the Long Bottom Ford parking area on the left.

DIFFICULTY	II (III-)
LENGTH	5.7 miles
PUT-IN	Long Bottom Ford
TAKE-OUT	Earl's Ford
ELEVATION	1581 to 1496
GRADIENT	15 fmp
DRAINAGE	66.5 sq. mi.
GAUGE	US 76 Bridge / USGS Chattooga
LEVELS	1'+

BETA

paddler andy hinton - andria baldovin photo

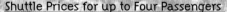

DIFFICULTY	III (IV)
LENGTH	12 miles
PUT-IN	Earl's Ford
TAKE-OUT	US 76
ELEVATION	1504 to 1207
GRADIENT	25 fpm
DRAINAGE	171 sq. mi.
GAUGE	76 Bridge or USGS
LEVELS	1' and up

BETA

Imagine a place so breathtakingly beautiful that you would happily give up a day of paddling to visit it. Now imagine that place with the best class III whitewater river in the Southeast running through it. Welcome to Section III—a spectacular Wild and Scenic River of clean clear water flowing through chutes, shoals, and over ledges and shelves lined with gigantic boulders and an unspoiled southern pine forest.

If you're up for the long day, put in at Earl's Ford and run down through the upper three miles to Sandy Ford, enjoying the shoals and chutes of Warwoman Rapid and the Beautiful Rock Garden shown in Deliverance. When you see Dick's Creek cascading down a waterfall into the river on the right, get out and scout the complicated shelf at Dick's Creek Ledge from the rocks in the middle.

Below here is Sandy Ford—an alternate put in for folks looking for a little bit shorter day. From Sandy Ford, the river flows down through the beautiful Narrows, with three distinct rapids and tall rock walls. Shortly below the Narrows, pull out on the left before a horizon line to scout the vertical drop of Second Ledge—many a paddler's first experience with vertical boating. Below here the river flows through countless fun rapids on its way to the grand finale—Class IV Bull Sluice—found right above the takeout and the Highway 76 bridge. You can scout this drop by following a short trail from the take out parking lot before driving up to put in. If you decide against the pre-boating scout, get out high above the drop on river right to scout or portage.

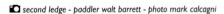
📷 *second ledge - paddler walt barrett - photo mark calcagni*

Shuttle: From the 76 bridge, drive east 100 yards and make a left into the parking area for the take out. To reach the put in, drive east on 76 2 miles to Chattooga Ridge Road on the left. Go 5.85 miles on Chattooga Ridge to a left at the stop sign at Earl's Ford Road. For the upper put in, drive straight to the end of Earl's Ford Road and walk down the trail to the river. For the short put in, take Earl's Ford Road to a left on 721-A after the horse use area. Follow this road to the parking lot and walk down the trail to the river.

📷 *bull sluice double drop @ 2.5 ft. - paddler andria baldovin - ©LD*

📷 *the narrows - paddler andria baldovin - ©LD*

89

31 · CHATTOOGA - SECTION IV ·

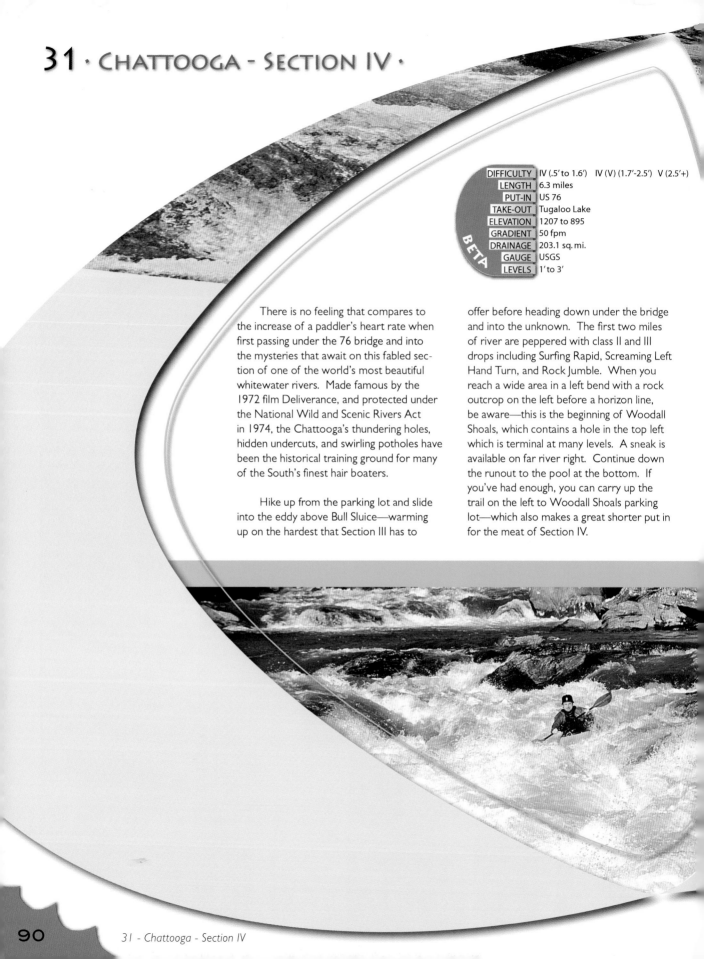

DIFFICULTY	IV (.5' to 1.6') IV (V) (1.7'-2.5') V (2.5'+)
LENGTH	6.3 miles
PUT-IN	US 76
TAKE-OUT	Tugaloo Lake
ELEVATION	1207 to 895
GRADIENT	50 fpm
DRAINAGE	203.1 sq. mi.
GAUGE	USGS
LEVELS	1' to 3'

BETA

There is no feeling that compares to the increase of a paddler's heart rate when first passing under the 76 bridge and into the mysteries that await on this fabled section of one of the world's most beautiful whitewater rivers. Made famous by the 1972 film Deliverance, and protected under the National Wild and Scenic Rivers Act in 1974, the Chattooga's thundering holes, hidden undercuts, and swirling potholes have been the historical training ground for many of the South's finest hair boaters.

Hike up from the parking lot and slide into the eddy above Bull Sluice—warming up on the hardest that Section III has to offer before heading down under the bridge and into the unknown. The first two miles of river are peppered with class II and III drops including Surfing Rapid, Screaming Left Hand Turn, and Rock Jumble. When you reach a wide area in a left bend with a rock outcrop on the left before a horizon line, be aware—this is the beginning of Woodall Shoals, which contains a hole in the top left which is terminal at many levels. A sneak is available on far river right. Continue down the runout to the pool at the bottom. If you've had enough, you can carry up the trail on the left to Woodall Shoals parking lot—which also makes a great shorter put in for the meat of Section IV.

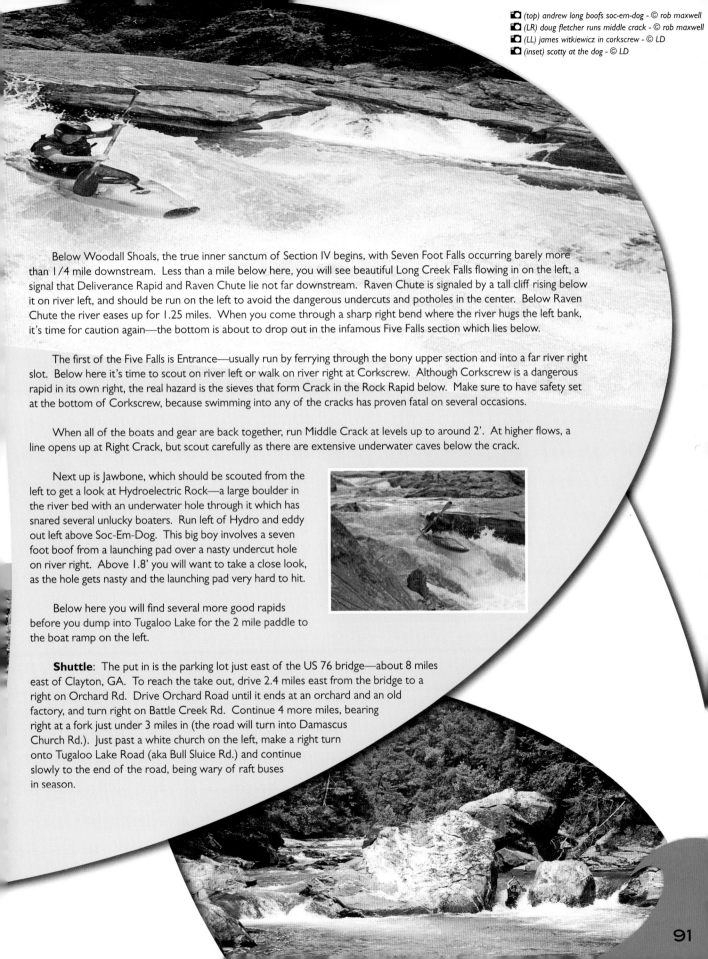

Below Woodall Shoals, the true inner sanctum of Section IV begins, with Seven Foot Falls occurring barely more than 1/4 mile downstream. Less than a mile below here, you will see beautiful Long Creek Falls flowing in on the left, a signal that Deliverance Rapid and Raven Chute lie not far downstream. Raven Chute is signaled by a tall cliff rising below it on river left, and should be run on the left to avoid the dangerous undercuts and potholes in the center. Below Raven Chute the river eases up for 1.25 miles. When you come through a sharp right bend where the river hugs the left bank, it's time for caution again—the bottom is about to drop out in the infamous Five Falls section which lies below.

The first of the Five Falls is Entrance—usually run by ferrying through the bony upper section and into a far river right slot. Below here it's time to scout on river left or walk on river right at Corkscrew. Although Corkscrew is a dangerous rapid in its own right, the real hazard is the sieves that form Crack in the Rock Rapid below. Make sure to have safety set at the bottom of Corkscrew, because swimming into any of the cracks has proven fatal on several occasions.

When all of the boats and gear are back together, run Middle Crack at levels up to around 2'. At higher flows, a line opens up at Right Crack, but scout carefully as there are extensive underwater caves below the crack.

Next up is Jawbone, which should be scouted from the left to get a look at Hydroelectric Rock—a large boulder in the river bed with an underwater hole through it which has snared several unlucky boaters. Run left of Hydro and eddy out left above Soc-Em-Dog. This big boy involves a seven foot boof from a launching pad over a nasty undercut hole on river right. Above 1.8' you will want to take a close look, as the hole gets nasty and the launching pad very hard to hit.

Below here you will find several more good rapids before you dump into Tugaloo Lake for the 2 mile paddle to the boat ramp on the left.

Shuttle: The put in is the parking lot just east of the US 76 bridge—about 8 miles east of Clayton, GA. To reach the take out, drive 2.4 miles east from the bridge to a right on Orchard Rd. Drive Orchard Road until it ends at an orchard and an old factory, and turn right on Battle Creek Rd. Continue 4 more miles, bearing right at a fork just under 3 miles in (the road will turn into Damascus Church Rd.). Just past a white church on the left, make a right turn onto Tugaloo Lake Road (aka Bull Sluice Rd.) and continue slowly to the end of the road, being wary of raft buses in season.

32 · TALLULAH GORGE ·

Since it opened to paddlers in 1997, Tallulah Gorge has quickly become one of the most loved runs in the Southeast. The combination of juicy class IV creeking, unmatched scenery, easy access, and shuttle service have created a following for this fine run and a new whitewater scene where there once was only a dry riverbed.

Park in the well marked "Boater Parking" area, and walk under the bridge and along the trail to the check in point at the rim of the gorge. Sign the waiver offered by the friendly volunteers, and head down the monster flight of 592 stairs to the put in. Make sure to walk on your heels and not your toes, or you'll be stuck with some jittery "Tallulah Legs" for several days after the run. Putting in, the action starts right away with Last Step—a solid class IV rapid that has caused many paddlers' Tallulah runs to start with a swim. Tanner's Boof follows on the right—head for the river left side at the end of the long pool and get out to scout Oceana.

Oceana is the monster drop of this run—a screaming fast 60 foot slide through "the Thing"—a massive explosion of water created by a rock ridge—and into a huge hole. This rapid has caused quite a few lacerations and broken legs, so make sure you're up to it

BETA	
DIFFICULTY	IV (V)
LENGTH	1.4 miles
PUT-IN	Tallulah Falls
TAKE-OUT	Tugaloo Lake
ELEVATION	1224 to 895
GRADIENT	207, 122
DRAINAGE	first 2 weekends in April, first 3 weekends in Nov.
GAUGE	Dam Release
LEVELS	500 cfs on Saturdays, 700 cfs on Sundays

before giving it a go. If you decide to wait for next time, ferry across the pool for the easier portage on river right.

Below Oceana there is some class II/III boogie, which turns into the class IV Gauntlet. Make sure and get an eddy at the end of Gauntlet, since Bridal Veil waits just below. It's best to head over to river left and get out when you see the horizon line. Bridal Veil is a fairly easy slide ending in a hole that is practically sucking the leaves off the nearby trees. Run the slide on the far left, or take the easy walk on that side.

From here Tallulah has many more fine class IV rapids down to the lake, where you should paddle straight across a little over 1.5 miles to the take out ramp to the right of the dam. Walk up and catch the shuttle ride back to your car at the put in.

Shuttle: Drive US 441 South of Clayton about 12 miles to the bridge over the Tallulah River and Dam. Park in the obvious boater parking area, just south of the bridge. There is a shuttle provided on release days, so put in and enjoy the ride!

AMERICAN
AW
WHITEWATER

entering the thing - paddler leland - photo eric young
a busy day on the stairs - photo brad roberts
bridal veil - photo brad roberts
oceana from above - © rob maxwell
andy o'reilly runs the middle line at oceana - © LD

93

shredding oceana - ricochet and amy - © LD

The Tallulah River has quickly become renowned for its spectacular whitewater, majestic gorge, and the close community of paddlers that frequent it. For nearly 80 years, however, the river once known as the "Niagara of the South" stood completely dry, with flows only after torrential floods or for the occasional Hollywood shoot.

In 1993, the attention of the entire region was once again focused on the Tallulah as American Whitewater conducted a flow study to test the viability of whitewater releases in the Gorge. An expert team of paddlers—Jerry Jascomb, Mike Hipsher, Nolan Whitesell, Kent Wigington, Ron Stewart, Jim Silavent, Mark Levine, John Bell, Charles Brewer, Bill Hester, and Walt Lynch—gathered at the Tallulah for the first descent.

Thanks to the extremely hard work of then—AW Executive Director Rich Bowers, American Whitewater volunteers Ron Stewart, Kent Wiggington, David Cox, Risa Shimoda, Woody Callaway, Rainy Hoffman, David Wallace, Sherry Olson, and Marshall Wilson, and our affiliate clubs the Atlanta Whitewater Club and the Georgia Canoe Association, the mighty Tallulah was freed in a monumental relicensing agreement that guaranteed 10 days of flows per year starting in November 1997 and created Tallulah Gorge State Park, conserving over 2,600 acres surrounding the Gorge.

Due to continued efforts by American Whitewater on the Tallulah, the competitive permit system—under which paddlers had to apply in groups for a permit months in advance in hopes of receiving one permit for one release day per season and which capped river usage at only 120 boaters per day—was removed in 2001 and now allows for completely open boating access. Since then, the Tallulah averages 250 boaters per day.

American Whitewater is currently working with Georgia Power and the Tallulah Gorge State Park on establishing up to 14 additional releases per year on the Tallulah. And to celebrate all of American Whitewater's efforts on the Tallulah, AW volunteers organize the annual "THING at the Tallulah Grassroots BBQ and Amateur Film Fest" during the November releases, with 100% of the proceeds going to American Whitewater.

Since American Whitewater relicensed the Tallulah and flows began again in 1997, the Tallulah has seamlessly brought together a large utility company, whitewater boaters, and an entire local community. Thanks to American Whitewater volunteers just like you and the continued responsible stewardship of the Gorge by its boaters, the Tallulah will continue to flow and be enjoyed for many more years to come.

Sutton Bacon

paddler sutton bacon

BOATERS ONLY

Franklin

Peeks
Creek
Road

Lower

Cullasaja
Falls

Middle

T-Bone

Bricklayer
Falls

Nemesis

US 64

Dry
Falls

Upper

Old
Mill
House

Lake
Sequoyah

Cashiers

HIGHLANDS

NC 108

NC

lower cullasaja - paddler chris stafford - ©LD

· CULLASAJA RIVER ·

upper cullasaja cascade - paddler brandon roy - ©LD

lower cullasaja - paddler charlie beavers - ©LD

33

· UPPER CULLASAJA ·

This short little run starts with a bang! The first drop is a towering 40 foot 3 stage cascade, and the action stays intense for a short ways below. Many folks just park and huck this awesome drop which is hidden in the rhododendron just below the dam. If you continue down, you'll find a notable mandatory portage about 1/4 mile downstream, and several more technical class V rapids as you make your way to Dry Falls.

A run over Dry Falls would be certain death, so scout your take out before driving up to put on.

Shuttle: Drive west on US 64 from Highlands to a pullout just past the end of Lake Sequoia. Put in at the base of the dam. To reach the take out, drive west about 1.25 miles to the Dry Falls parking area.

BETA	
DIFFICULTY	V+
LENGTH	1.3 miles
PUT-IN	Just below Lake Sequoyah
TAKE-OUT	Just above Dry Falls
ELEVATION	3610 to 3346
GRADIENT	231 (214 in 1/2 mile), 33
DRAINAGE	14.1 sq. mi.
GAUGE	USGS Culasaja R. Near Highlands
LEVELS	4.0' to 5'

📷 (UR) 1st cascade - paddler brandon roy - ©LD
📷 (Middle) cheezer heads downstream - ©LD
📷 (Bottom) jj shepherd searches for answers
(and his paddle) in the 1st cascade - ©LD

34 · MIDDLE CULLASAJA ·

pat keller on bricklayer falls - ©pisgahwhitewater.com

BETA	
DIFFICULTY	IV (V)
LENGTH	2.8 miles
PUT-IN	Below Cosmic Crunch
TAKE-OUT	Above Cullasaja Falls
ELEVATION	2929 to 2639
GRADIENT	142,52,96
DRAINAGE	24.6 sq. mi.
GAUGE	USGS Culasaja R. Near Highlands
LEVELS	3.5' to 5'

cheezer t-bonin' for the ladies - ©LD

The Middle Cullasaja is an excellent roadside class IV creek run for those looking to step up their adventure level into the creeking arena. It features some moderate gradient at the beginning, a flatter stretch in the middle, and some greater gradient just before the end. It is mostly road scoutable and easy to exit from, with large pools at the end of most of the major drops.

Scramble down the bank and put on below Cosmic Crunch—a large horrible looking 30 foot drop. This is the end of the extreme section of the middle—with massive drops such as Nemesis and Bricklayer Falls that have dished out severe beatings to some of the world's best creek boaters. Paddle down from here through the rapids and ledges, being wary of the scout above T-bone, the biggest rapid on the run which is clearly visible from the road on the drive up. Below here, there is another good stretch of whitewater down to a take out above Cullasaja Falls. The difficulty gets much harder and the eddies much more scarce just above the falls—and a run over the falls would be certain death—so scout your takeout carefully when you run shuttle to avoid any accidents.

Shuttle: Take 64 East from Franklin or West from Highlands into the Cullasaja Gorge. Choose a pullout upstream of Cullasaja Falls and scout your take out. For the put in, drive 2.75 miles East on 64 and find another pullout. Walk down the steep hill to the river.

35 · LOWER CULLASAJA ·

DIFFICULTY	V/V+
LENGTH	1 mile
PUT-IN	Cullasaja Falls
TAKE-OUT	SR 1678
ELEVATION	2432 to 2133
GRADIENT	299
DRAINAGE	34.1 sq. mi.
GAUGE	USGS
LEVELS	3.4' to 4.4'

BETA

📷 *danny mongno dropping in - photo johan forsberg*

The Lower Cullasaja is a steep but technical classic—the perfect training run for class V+ like the Raven Fork. Dropping a car at the Peeks Creek bridge, you'll wonder how this innocent looking little stream can pack that much punch. When you pull over on the narrow pullout high above the falls, it will all be clear. Walking down the steep gully to the river you might start having second thoughts—and for good reason.

What it lacks in length the Cullasaja makes up for with gnar—dropping precipitously through the first 4 class V and V+ drops before mellowing to moderate class V- boogie through a short mid section and crashing down two more sizeable class Vs at the end. All drops should be carefully scouted on this run, and the third and fourth drops are very frequently walked. The third drop is known as Ecplise—so named because it Eclipses Sunshine on the Green in difficulty, and the fourth is known as Maybe Next Time. The second to last drop—Trash Can—is a mandatory portage on river right since the floods of 2004 rearranged the rapid. After the final drop of Whale's Tail, hurry through the class III/IV runout for the final half mile so you can make it back up for another lap.

Shuttle: Take US 64 east from Franklin or west from Highlands into the Cullasaja Gorge. Pull out on the narrow shoulder overlooking Cullasaja Falls, and walk down the steep rocky gully to the put in at the base. To reach the take out, head west from the falls just under 1.5 miles to the first left on Peeks Creek Road. Drive down Peeks Creek a short distance and park near the bridge.

📷 *second drop - paddler chris stafford - ©LD*

eclipse - paddlers chris stafford and nate elliot - ©LD

CENTRAL
MOUNTAINS

pat keller in quarry rapid - ©LD

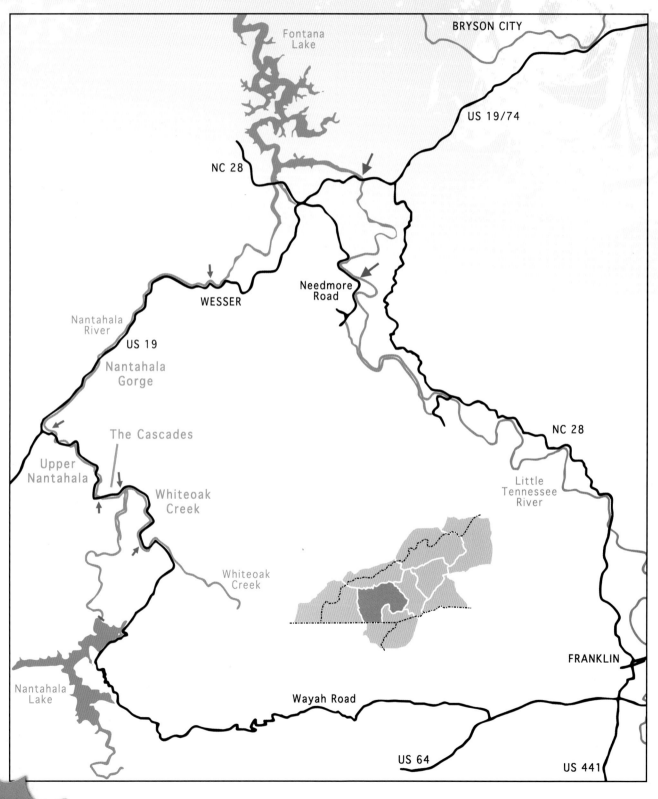

BRYSON CITY

Fontana Lake

US 19/74

NC 28

WESSER

Needmore Road

Nantahala River

US 19

Nantahala Gorge

NC 28

The Cascades

Upper Nantahala

Little Tennessee River

Whiteoak Creek

Whiteoak Creek

FRANKLIN

Nantahala Lake

Wayah Road

US 64

US 441

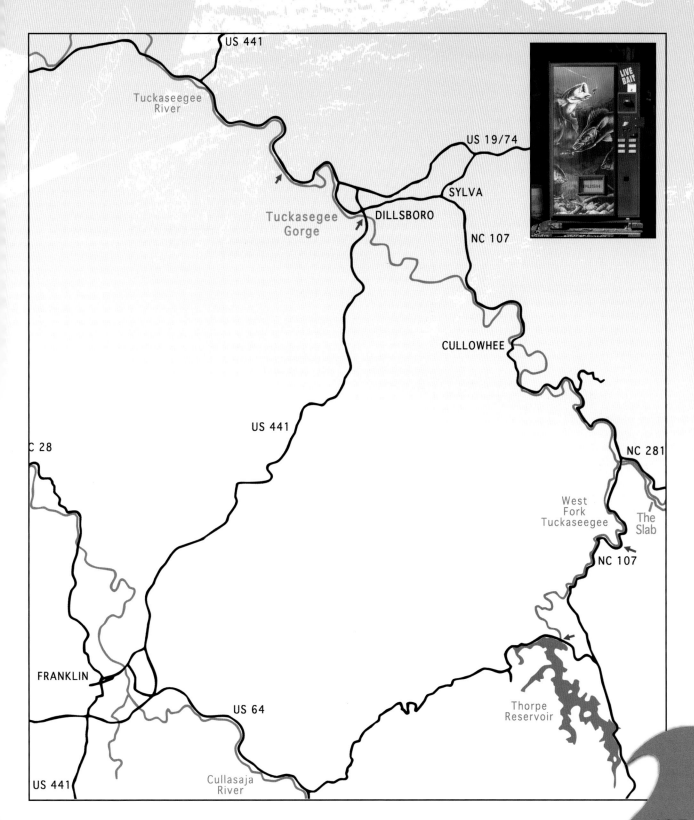

US 441

Tuckaseegee
River

US 19/74

SYLVA

Tuckasegee
Gorge

DILLSBORO

NC 107

CULLOWHEE

C 28

US 441

NC 281

West
Fork
Tuckaseegee

The
Slab

NC 107

FRANKLIN

US 64

Thorpe
Reservoir

US 441

Cullasaja
River

DIFFICULTY	III/IV
LENGTH	6.2 miles
PUT-IN	Thorpe Dam
TAKE-OUT	Power Plant
ELEVATION	3238 to 2286
GRADIENT	427, 63, 169, 148, 74, 53, 18
SEASON	1 late Apr. Wkend, 5 wkend days May - Sept.
GAUGE	Dam Release
LEVELS	250 cfs 10am - 4pm

This fun little stream is soon to be one of AW's great successes and a fantastic addition to the growing southeastern dam release circuit. Dewatered for over 60 years by the power plant, the West Fork will run again by 2006 due to a relicensing agreement negotiated by American Whitewater.

Walking to the bottom of the dam at Thorpe Reservoir, paddlers will put in on a beautiful stream shaded by overhanging forests and winding over slides and small rapids through a tunnel of rhododendron. There will be one major portage at High Falls, and then the action begins in earnest about 1/2 mile downstream with a 20 foot rapid which can be run as a slide on river left or a tricky near vertical drop on the right. Below this slide, the river continues with miles of fun class II and III, a little class IV thrown in for spice, and one fairly solid class IV toward the end. Be aware that the land bordering the stream is private property, and make all efforts to stay below the high water mark if you must leave your boat.

Releases will be on a schedule of one full weekend in late April, and five more weekend days between May 1st and September 30th—giving a great summer option for aspiring creek boaters looking for a change of scenery from the Upper Green. The beginning of releases is contingent on completion of the access parking lots and portage trail, so check the American Whitewater website for updates on the status of this run—and make sure to join and support AW so that they can continue the fight to open up great creeks like the West Fork!

Shuttle: From Cullowhee, drive about 10 miles south on 107 to the take out parking area which is planned near the power plant. For the put in, continue up 107 another 5 miles to a right turn to Thorpe Dam. Drive to the dam and park in the planned designated parking area.

ken kastorff by kevin colburn

the big one

barry kennon throws down by lamp light - © pisgahwhitewater.com

This fine little play hole is the brain child and training ground of 2001 world champion freestyle C-1er Barry Kennon. Tucked away on the East Fork of the Tuckasegee just outside of Cullowhee, this little hole offers ends and blunts to the patient paddler, as well as the occasional loop to the local hero.   Being human modified, this feature comes and goes with the floods and high flows, so ask around about the status before you travel too far to surf. Work has also been ongoing on a pourover hole just downstream, so check both locations if you go.

Gauges and Levels: Release Information at 866-332-5253, 200 - 300 cfs is optimal.

Shuttle: From Cullowhee, drive south on 107 just under 7 miles until you cross the East Fork. Make a left just past the East Fork, and continue up the road about 1.5 miles to a gravel pullout on the right. Walk down the steep slope to the river and the hole just downstream.

ryan bednar photo

38 · TUCKASEGEE ·

DIFFICULTY	II
LENGTH	4.4 miles
PUT-IN	Dillsboro
TAKE-OUT	Barkers Creek Rd.
ELEVATION	1951 to 1890
GRADIENT	14 fpm
SEASON	Year Round
GAUGE	USGS
LEVELS	800+

BETA

📷 © LD

With nice scenery, an easy shuttle, reliable releases and some really fun class I and II, the Tuckasegee offers a fantastic first moving water experience for the

aspiring whitewater addict. Although it can be urban at times, and the water is a trifle dirty from the town of Cullowhee upstream, the gorge has some great scenery and rapids which are lots of fun without posing any serious dangers.

Putting in at Dillsboro, float through some small rapids past hotels and other development, keeping an eye out on river right for the set from the train wreck scene of the 1993 Harrison Ford flick

"The Fugitive." Continue downstream until the railroad crosses the river—this is where the action picks up. From here down, the river is marked with well spaced class II rapids separated by pools and class I riffles with beautiful mountain views. There are several great places to stop and swim along the way, so take your time and enjoy your day.

Shuttle: To reach the git-out, drive 2.8 miles west on 19a/74 from the US 441 S/Dillsboro exit. Park at the far end of the outfitters lot which is just downstream of the Barkers Creek Rd. Bridge. Take out under the bridge and be respectful walking past the outfitters. To get to the git-in, return to 441 S to Dillsboro. After crossing the river in Dillsboro, make the first left and another immediate left. Go down the short hill, and make a left under the bridge before the train tracks into the parking area.

📷 © pisgahwhitewater.com

39 · LITTLE TENNESSEE ·

DIFFICULTY	II
LENGTH	6.5 miles
PUT-IN	Needmore Road
TAKE-OUT	Fontana Lake
ELEVATION	1762 to 1693
GRADIENT	11 fpm
DRAINAGE	Year Round natural flow / 439.4 sq. mi.
GAUGE	USGS or TVA Little Tennessee at Needmore
LEVELS	500 - 2000 cfs

BETA

📷 ©LD

The Little Tennessee is a fantastic class I/II float over wide shoal style rapids and ledges through a beautiful mountain valley. There is one significant class III rapid at the end during times of year (generally all but the summer months) when the lake is low enough to expose it. Just below this final rapid you will float out into Fontana Lake, continuing about a half mile until you pass under the US 19 bridge. Take out below the bridge on the right and walk up the old road to your car. Alternately, you can pick any section of the river which flows along Needmore Road for miles upstream.

Shuttle: To reach the take out, drive west 6 miles from Bryson City on highway 19 to a pullout on the right just before the Capt. T.A. Sandlin Memorial Bridge over the Little Tennessee River (which is Fontana Lake at this point). To reach the put in, continue on 19 just over 2 miles to Needmore Road on the left. Take Needmore just over 2 miles to the river, or continue over another small ridge and access the river at a higher point.

40 · WHITEOAK CREEK ·

becky's - ©LD

DIFFICULTY	V (V+)
LENGTH	2 miles
PUT-IN	Whiteoak Dam
TAKE-OUT	Nantahala River
ELEVATION	3028 to 2623
GRADIENT	182, 223
DRAINAGE	13.8 sq. mi.
GAUGE	visual
LEVELS	

BETA

If it's raining in the Nantahala drainage and you're looking for more adventure than the Cascades have to offer, Whiteoak Creek may be your answer. Although it's not the highest quality run, Whiteoak boasts some interesting class IV creeking through overhanging rhododendron, with two large class V drops thrown in to keep you on your toes.

The first larger drop comes about half way through the run. This one was first run by former NOC employee Becky Weis—who was one of the first women to run the Green Narrows and also competed on the US free-style team in the early '90s. According to her story, she missed the eddy, threw her paddle on the bank, and was clawing at the dirt and moss on the riverbank with her fingernails to avoid running this "mandatory portage." Failing to stop, she washed through the entire rapid backwards without a paddle, cleaning the drop—now affectionately known as "Becky's Buttf*#k."

The final rapid on the run is Whiteoak Falls—also known as the Mean Mistreater. Run down the gut of the entrance chute, bank off the wall, and launch over the final vertical 15 footer—making sure to boof into the 2 feet or so of water at the base. This rapid has the potential to dish out hearty helpings of beat down, so think carefully before taking the plunge. If you've made it this far, you probably want to cool down with a run through the Cascades of the Nantahala directly below.

Shuttle: From NOC in Wesser, drive up the gorge to the first major left on Wayah Rd. at Beechertown. Head up along the river just over 4 miles to a road on the right below the Mean Mistreater. Park here for the take out. To reach the put in, continue up the paved road 2.4 miles to Whiteoak Dam.

mean mistreater - paddler pat keller - photo kevin colburn

41 · THE CASCADES ·

DIFFICULTY	IV/V
LENGTH	.6 miles
PUT-IN	Just downstream of Whiteoak Creek
TAKE-OUT	sr 1310 bridge
ELEVATION	2489 to 2350
GRADIENT	139
SEASON	1 WE late April, 4 AN summer, one WE late Sept. / 126.9 sq. mi.
GAUGE	release
LEVELS	250 - 425 cfs

BETA

📷 paddler pat keller - ©LD

The Cascades is a fantastic little stretch to run some laps on if the water's up in the Nantahala area. Usually only run after rain brings up Whiteoak Creek, these fantastic drops will see regular releases after 2006 thanks to the hard work of American Whitewater.

The entire run is roadside and visible from the car on the way up. Scout carefully on the drive—some of these get pretty meaty at high levels, and at low levels there exists lots of possibility for a pin. There are four rapids, with the first two—the Horns of God and Big Kahuna—being the biggest. Below this there are two more good drops, and then some runout to the bridge and your ride back up for another lap.

Starting in 2006, the river will run one weekend in late April from 10 - 4. The level will be 250 cfs on Saturday, and 350 cfs on Sunday. There will be four afternoons between June 15th and August 31st with releases of 250 cfs from 4 to 7. Finally, there will be another weekend of releases in late September, with a flow of 300 cfs on Saturday from 10 to 5. Sunday, the release will start out at 425 cfs from 10 to 3, and then taper to 250 cfs from 3 to 5. The release schedule will be posted in October for the following year at www.americanwhitewater.org.

Shuttle: From NOC in Wesser, drive up the gorge to the first major left on Wayah Rd. at Beechertown. Head up along the river for 3.25 miles to a pullout just before the road crosses to river right. For the git-in, continue up the road until a pullout upstream of the obvious cascading drops.

AMERICAN
AW
WHITEWATER

📷 the horns of god - paddler pat keller - ©LD

· NANTAHALA RIVER ·

Wesser Falls

Wesser

Nantahala
Falls

Quarry
Rapid

Nantahala Gorge

Quarry
Parking

Ferebee
Launch
Site

US 19

Nantahala River

Beechertown
Access

Andrews

NC 1310

Upper
Nantahala

Mean
Mistreater

The
Cascades

Whiteoak
Dam

Whiteoak Creek

Nantahala
Lake

©LD

DIFFICULTY	II/III (III+)
LENGTH	3.3 miles
PUT-IN	sr 1310 bridge
TAKE-OUT	Beechertown
ELEVATION	2348 to 1996
GRADIENT	155,93,99,5
SEASON	1 WE late April, 4 AN summer, one WE late Sept. / 127.1 sq. mi.
GAUGE	release
LEVELS	250 - 425 cfs

BETA

The Upper Nantahala is an excellent small step up from the popular gorge run below, and will flow on a regular schedule starting in 2006 due to a relicensing agreement negotiated by American Whitewater. The whole run is roadside class II/III, and is easily scouted from the car on the drive up. The one rapid of note is a sticky hole found under the first bridge below the put in—which is only a concern at higher levels.

Starting in 2006, the river will run one weekend in late April from 10 - 4. The level will be 250 cfs on Saturday, and 350 cfs on Sunday. There will be four afternoons between June 15th and August 31st with releases of 250 cfs from 4 to 7. Finally, there will be another weekend of releases in late September, with a flow of 300 cfs on Saturday from 10 to 5. Sunday, the release will start out at 425 cfs from 10 to 3, and then taper to 250 cfs from 3 to 5. This run is quite bony (but still runable) at 250 cfs, and should really only be considered on days with releases of at least 350 cfs.

Check the American Whitewater website for the latest updates on these releases.

Shuttle: From NOC in Wesser, drive up the gorge to the first major left on Wayah Rd. at Beechertown. Just after turning onto Wayah Rd. (Beechertown Rd.), make a left into the take out parking lot. To reach the put in, head up along the river for 3.25 miles to a pullout just before the road crosses to river right.

43 · NANTAHALA ·

The Nantahala Gorge from Beechertown to Wesser is the most paddled stretch of whitewater in the state—and for good reason. The birthplace of mass commercial rafting, home of several of the World's best kayaking schools, and training ground of olympic slalom racers, the Nantahala offers fast class II water with well defined eddies perfect for the learning kayaker. Although it's too difficult and cold to make a great first moving water experience, the Nantahala is the perfect place to step it up and improve your skills when the Lower Green, Hiwassee, and Tuckasegee have become a bit too easy. The thrill of running class III Nantahala Falls for your first time is sure to stick with you for the rest of your paddling career.

Putting in at Beechertown, you will find the river's second biggest rapid—Patton's Run—right around the first right bend. Stay to the inside of the turn. If you swim keep your feet up—several people have been killed by foot entrapments due to the rocky bottom and fast moving water in this rapid. Below this it's 2.5 miles down to the first highway bridge, and the lower put in at the Ferebee river access. A short distance downstream, head right of an island and look for the best playspot on the run—Quarry Hole—just below.

The other rapid of note is the final hoorah—Nantahala Falls—which is found right above the takeout and can be scouted when you run shuttle. This rapid has probably given more paddlers their first class III experience than any other, and also causes lots of first class III swims. Get out at the well marked take outs near the bridges downstream, being aware that there is a chunky man made class IV+ rapid about 100 yards below the first bridge. This drop—Wesser Falls—can be run if you're looking for one last thrill before the river joins Fontana Lake.

Shuttle: From the NOC in Wesser, drive West on 19 about 7.5 miles to the first major left on Wayah Rd. in Beechertown.   After turning, take an immediate left into the parking area. The takeout is at the NOC—please observe their most current postings and directions on where it is acceptable to park.

pattons run - ©LD

nantahala falls fantasy - ©LD

DIFFICULTY	II/III
LENGTH	7.8 miles
PUT-IN	Beechertown
TAKE-OUT	Wesser
ELEVATION	1990 to 1711
GRADIENT	36 fpm
SEASON	year round
GAUGE	828-488-2176, x426
LEVELS	on (586 cfs)

BETA

noc wave - © pisgahwhitewater.com

44 · QUARRY ·

pat keller - ©LD

Quarry hole is the best play spot in the area—if you can avoid the crowds and don't mind wearing your drytop in the middle of summer. The hole is custom crafted by local raft guides and gorge dwellers, so it comes and goes with the floods and the whims of the locals. A lot of folks have invested massive amounts of time figuring out what works here and what doesn't, so do not move the rocks around in the river bed—more often than not uneducated tinkering makes the hole worse or eliminates the eddy.

When the spot is in, it offers up just about any hole move you want—ends, blunts, loops, and other fun. The reliable dam releases allow for catching it at times when the raft traffic is low during mid week in the summer, or for most of the spring and winter when nobody else is around. No matter when you catch it, you're sure to want a trip back to this friendly fluffy fun spot.

Gage and levels: The Nantahala runs almost every day of the year, with the exception of the months of November and December. The release level is 586 cfs, and this will be the flow unless it's been raining and the tributaries are kicking in more water. Call the NOC water line at 828-488-2176, x426 to find out the release.

Shuttle: From the NOC in Wesser, drive West on 19 just over 4.5 miles to a pullout on the right about 1/4 mile before the Ferebee River access. Park and walk down to the river. Head downstream to the playspot, keeping to the main (right) channel when the river splits.

· MYSTERY CREEK ·

DIFFICULTY	V?
LENGTH	2.5 miles
PUT-IN	Mystery Creek Road
TAKE-OUT	Mystery Creek Road
ELEVATION	3562 to 2707
GRADIENT	364, 361, 130
DRAINAGE	5.6 sq. mi.
GAUGE	visual
LEVELS	

BETA

Mystery Creek is a beautiful stream tucked away in a dark corner of North Carolina, and it has never been paddled. This book will lead you to an abundance of phenominal rivers, but remember that there are plenty of new adventures to be had out there as well. Never stop exploring!

WESTERN
MOUNTAINS

📷 *hell hole - paddler chris stafford - ©LD*

US 129

Calderwood Res.

NC 28

Citico Creek

Slickrock Creek

Cheoah Res.

Fontana Lake

Cheoah River

Yellow Creek

TELLICO PLAINS

Cherohala Skyway

Santeetlah Lake

Santeetlah Creek

NC 143

Tellico River

ROBBINS-VILLE

Snowbird Creek

US 129

Coker Creek

RELIANCE

ANDREWS

Hiwassee River

Appalachia Lake

US 19/74

TN 30

TN 68

Lake Ocoee

Ocoee River

US 64

Ocoee #3 Lake

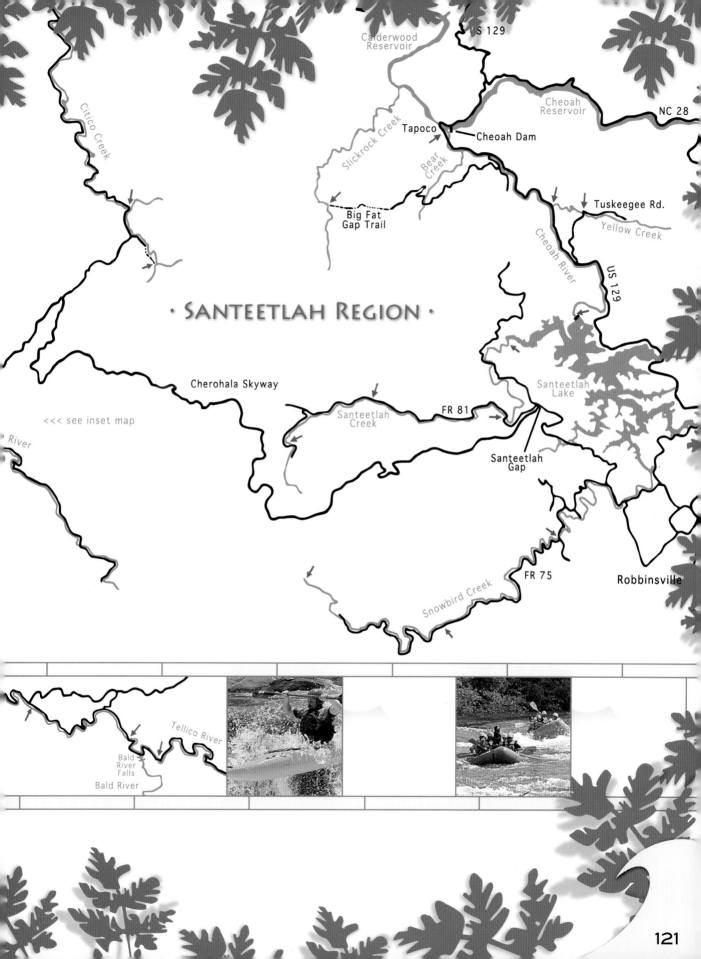

· SANTEETLAH REGION ·

Calderwood Reservoir

US 129

Cheoah Reservoir

NC 28

Citico Creek

Slickrock Creek

Tapoco

Cheoah Dam

Bear Creek

Big Fat Gap Trail

Tuskeegee Rd.

Yellow Creek

Cheoah River

US 129

Cherohala Skyway

<<< see inset map

Santeetlah Creek

FR 81

Santeetlah Lake

River

Santeetlah Gap

FR 75

Snowbird Creek

Robbinsville

Tellico River

Bald River Falls

Bald River

45 · UPPER SNOWBIRD ·

DIFFICULTY	IV
LENGTH	6.65 miles
PUT-IN	Hooper Bald
TAKE-OUT	Junction
ELEVATION	3743 to 2696
GRADIENT	87, 123, 146, 153, 228, 184, 126
DRAINAGE	3.2 sq. mi.
GAUGE	AFWS Chestnut Flats / Tellico River
LEVELS	3"+ in 6 hours / 5'+

BETA

Upper Snowbird Creek is a run that remains shrouded in mystery, and to some extent I'm sure it will always be that way. The creek has a long shuttle, a long hike in, and requires a tremendous amount of water to get it running. Despite all of those things, any run which requires dropping off the Cherohala Skyway into a pristine wilderness to put in has got to be worth the trouble.

Although I have not run Upper Snowbird at the time of this writing, reports I have received indicate that the run is class III/IV with 4 larger waterfalls, three of which are clearly marked on the topo map, and all of which are said to be runable. From the pictures I've seen, Upper Falls and Big Falls are both double tiered sliding drops, while Middle Falls is a clean 20 foot vertical into a big pool. The final falls, which are not on the map, also are mostly sliding.

Look for very high water at the take out before attempting to put on—Upper Snowbird is a long day, and the water will drop quickly while you're on the creek. Drive up to the Cherohala Skyway and park in the Hooper Bald parking area. Walk .1 miles on the Hooper Bald Trail and turn right on King Meadows Trail (Trail #63). Take King Meadows Trail to Mitchell Lick Trail (#154). Follow Mitchell Lick Trail 1.5 miles to the creek, and hike downstream until it gets big enough to put on.

Shuttle: From the Subway/Texaco in Robbinsville, head north on 129 1.4 miles to a left turn signed to Joyce Kilmer and the Cherohala Skyway. Follow this road about 3.4 miles until it ends, and turn right onto NC 1127. Continue a little over 2 miles to Snowbird Rd. on the left. Follow Snowbird Rd. just over 2 more miles, and make a left to stay on Snowbird Rd. Continue until you cross the creek, and bear right where Snowbird and Little Snowbird Creeks split. Continue to the end of the road and leave a take out vehicle. To reach the put in, return to NC 1127 and go left. Continue a little over 4.5 miles to Santeetlah Gap, and get on the Cherohala Skyway. Follow the Skyway to the Hooper Bald parking area and trailhead.

46 · LOWER SNOWBIRD ·

Lower Snowbird is a fantastic class III/IV roadside romp through a beautiful little gorge. The bulk of the gradient is in the section just below Junction, but the rest of the creek is incredibly scenic as well. The rapids tend to be boulder style, with small rocks and continuous flow reminiscent of creeking in the Great Smokies National Park. The road is directly along the creek, so it is possible to choose any put in or take out that suits you.

Shuttle: From the Subway/Texaco in Robbinsville, head north on 129 1.4 miles to a left turn signed to Joyce Kilmer and the Cherohala Skyway. Follow this road about 3.4 miles until it ends, and turn right onto NC 1127. Continue a little over 2 miles to Snowbird Rd. on the left. Follow Snowbird Rd. just over 2 more miles, and make a left to stay on Snowbird Rd. Continue until you cross the creek, and bear right where Snowbird and Little Snowbird Creeks split. Leave the takeout vehicle at the end of the field where the National Forest begins. Continue to the put in at the end of the road.

DIFFICULTY	IV
LENGTH	6 miles
PUT-IN	Junction
TAKE-OUT	SR 1115
ELEVATION	2694 to 2114
GRADIENT	153,128,132,69,42,56
DRAINAGE	12.7 sq. mi.
GAUGE	AFWS Chestnut Flats / Tellico R.
LEVELS	2"+ rain in 6 hours / 4'+

BETA

paddler john pilson - © LD

47 · UPPER SANTEETLAH ·

BETA

DIFFICULTY	V
LENGTH	2.64 miles
PUT-IN	Whigg Branch
TAKE-OUT	Roadside - below gate
ELEVATION	3838 to 2922
GRADIENT	249, 415, 252
DRAINAGE	4.7 sq. mi.
GAUGE	AFWS Chestnut Flats / Tellico River
LEVELS	2"+ / 4'+

Upper Santeetlah is a hard to catch creeking classic, sure to be a favorite of anyone who does make it down this spectacular run. Draining from high in an unspoiled wilderness area, this run slides, drops, and rushes through a misty forest thick with rhododendron and peppered with old growth hemlocks. You'll only notice the scenery while scouting, though, because the incredible rapids of Santeetlah will keep you focused while you're on the creek. Putting in at the Whigg Branch Confluence, paddlers will wind through a rocky first section for about a half mile, portaging wood as necessary. Beyond this the bedrock starts, containing many fun slides culminating with The Hallway, a very long low angle slide between a sloping slab on the left and a vertical wall on the right.

Not too far below the hallway is the biggest drop on the run—a trashy 25 foot cascade which has seen a few runs on the right, but more often is carried left. Below this the difficulty picks up, with alternating slides, large boulder rapids, and vertical drops for a while—all of which are super high quality. Be careful to scout often, since wood can be an issue in this small creek. You'll know the end is coming when the creek changes to continuous boulder boogie reminiscent of the West Prong. Make sure you walk to the river and get a visual of the take out before putting on, because it's easy to miss from the creek.

Shuttle: From the Subway/Texaco in Robbinsville, head north on 129 1.4 miles to a left turn signed to Joyce Kilmer and the Cherohala Skyway. Follow this road about 3.4 miles until it ends, and turn right onto NC 1127. Continue a little over 6.5 miles to Santeetlah Gap, and make a right and then an immediate left onto forest road 81. Follow FR 81 down to the creek, cross the bridge, and continue upstream to a gate about 4-5 miles in. Leave the take out vehicle here, and continue upstream, bearing left at the fork in the road before a small bridge and then parking at the next bridge.

paddler robin betz - © LD

paddler donnie kemp -©LD

the hallway - paddler andria baldovin - © LD

48 · MIDDLE SANTEETLAH ·

paddler matt jennings - photo wayne dickert

Middle Santeetlah is a great roadside option for folks wanting to experience the beauty of the creek without the hair raising rapids found on the upper stretch. The river is roadside with easy access at both ends, but it falls away from the road in the middle section—allowing for a more wild feeling. Wood often collects in this stream, so keep your eyes open on the way down.

BETA	
DIFFICULTY	III/IV
LENGTH	4.7 miles
PUT-IN	Roadside- Below gate
TAKE-OUT	FS 81 Bridge
ELEVATION	2916 to 2235
GRADIENT	230,182,150,76,43
DRAINAGE	11.8 sq.mi.
GAUGE	AFWS Chestnut Flats / Tellico R.
LEVELS	2"+ / 4'+

Shuttle: From the Subway/Texaco in Robbinsville, head north on 129 1.4 miles to a left turn signed to Joyce Kilmer and the Cherohala Skyway. Follow this road about 3.4 miles until it ends, and turn right onto NC 1127. Continue a little over 6.5 miles to Santeetlah Gap, and make a right and then an immediate left onto forest road 81. Follow FR 81 down to the creek, cross the bridge, and drop the take out vehicle. Continue upstream to a gate about 4-5 miles in for the put in.

49 · LOWER SANTEETLAH ·

paddler anne sontheimer - photo wayne dickert

Lower Santeetlah is a fun little intro to creeking in a beautiful area adjacent to the Joyce Kilmer Memorial Forest. The top section, from FR 81 down to the first bridge is class II/III, with lots of fun little rapids for beginning creekers. Below the bridge at SR 1127, the river will pick up pace. The first item of note is a low head dam—be wary of this feature, and get out well in advance to portage. Below here the rapids will be sprinkled with class III/IV, with several fun drops down to the take out at the lake.

Shuttle: From the Subway/Texaco in Robbinsville, head north on 129 1.4 miles to a left turn signed to Joyce Kilmer and the Cherohala Skyway. Follow this road about 3.4 miles until it ends, and turn right onto NC 1127. Continue a little over 6.5 miles to Santeetlah Gap, and make a right to continue on NC 1127. Go 2.25 miles to a right turn after the bridge over Santeetlah Creek. Follow this road a short distance and pull out at the beginning of the lake. To reach the put in, return to Santeetlah Gap and make a right on FR 81, driving down the hill to the bridge over the creek.

BETA	
DIFFICULTY	III
LENGTH	3.8 miles
PUT-IN	FS 81 Bridge
TAKE-OUT	Santeetlah Lake
ELEVATION	2236 to 1963
GRADIENT	72 fpm
DRAINAGE	20.1 sq.mi.
GAUGE	AFWS Chestnut Flats / Tellico R.
LEVELS	2"+ / 4'+

50 · YELLOW CREEK ·

DIFFICULTY	IV/V
LENGTH	1.25 miles
PUT-IN	Yellow Creek Road
TAKE-OUT	Cheoah River
ELEVATION	1818 to 1456
GRADIENT	290 fpm
DRAINAGE	12.6 sq. mi.
GAUGE	USGS Cheoah at Bearpen Gap
LEVELS	200+ cfs

BETA

charlie dillon drops the big one - photo kevin colburn

Yellow Creek is arguably one of the best kept secrets in Western North Carolina. If you have heard of it, the first thing you'll hear it called is the easiest 290 fpm creek in North Carolina. But that's not to say it's easy.

Over the course of little over a mile, this micro creek contains some big slides, a clean 20 footer, and some wonderful boulder garden drops in a lower section that drops at a rate of 600 fpm. Overall, it's a solid IV/V and while it may not be a destination creek like the nearby Upper Santeetlah, Yellow is definitely worth checking out the day after a big rain when you are in the area. Yes, the day after. Perhaps the best part of Yellow Creek is its 13 square mile drainage with farmlands up at the top. It doesn't take much rain to get going, and then it often holds its water and tends to run after everything else drops down.

At first glance from the take out the creek seems incredibly micro, but a short 15 yard hike upstream reveals a beautiful little gorge. From there, you can either hike up the clearly marked trail to the 20 footer for some quick park n' huck or put in all the way at the top off Yellow Creek Road. If you do plan to put in at the top, I suggest hiking from the bottom at least up to the falls for a quick scout of it and the notable sieve in the second boulder garden rapid following the slides below the falls.

When the USGS Cheoah gauge spikes, that means Yellow is running. Unfortunately, we need more runs reported to determine accurate correlations between the online gauge and the culvert gauge, but look for at least 200 cfs before heading over there. If you do catch Yellow on a good water day, go ahead and set shuttle at the bottom of the Cheoah, either near Tapoco Lodge

or at the lake. If Yellow is running well, then you can do a low-water tour of the Cheoah's steepest section.

Thanks to American Whitewater's efforts during the Cheoah River relicensing, the Yellow Creek Gorge has been protected from commercial development. A significant buffer will be established that protects the creek and our right to access it, and AW will continue working to protect this creek and improve its water quality.

Sutton Bacon

Shuttle: From the Texaco/Subway in Robbinsville, drive 11.25 miles north on US 129 to the take out where Yellow Creek passes under the road and into the Cheoah. Backtrack about 2 miles south on 129, and make a left on Yellow Creek Rd., proceeding just under 2 miles to the put in at the bridge over the creek.

51 · CHEOAH ·

📷 paddler hank zachary - © LD (R eye)

📷 paddlers ken strickland & hank zachary - © LD (tooth L)

📷 paddler ken strickland - © LD (tooth R)

📷 paddlers ken strickland & hank zachary - © LD (L eye)

📷 paddler ken strickland - © LD (below)

DIFFICULTY	IV
LENGTH	9.25 miles
PUT-IN	Santeetlah Dam
TAKE-OUT	Calderwood Lake
ELEVATION	1766 to 1087
GRADIENT	42,51,52,109,77,58,38,106,146
SEASON	Releases/ 174.1 sq. mi.
GAUGE	USGS Cheoah nr. Tapoco
LEVELS	500 - 2500

BETA

AMERICAN
AW
WHITEWATER

Idaho called. Seems they're missing a few miles of river, and they think it wound up in the Cheoah Valley. With fairly constant gradient, continuous big water rapids, and fun catch-on-the-fly waves, this treasure is a little piece of Idaho whitewater lurking in a forgotten corner of Appalachia. Cheoah has many good big water rapids, some fun play, and a roadside ease of use that makes it a must do for any southern boater.

Any section from Santeetlah Lake to Cheoah Reservoir can be run, but the most common run is the final couple of miles from the FS road bridge over the river down to the Res. This section contains most of the more difficult whitewater, boasting several large class III and IV rapids.

This riverbed has been dewatered for many years by the hydro plant, but thanks to the efforts of American Whitewater, the relicensing of this dam will provide recreational releases through this excellent river by 2005 or 2006. The plan calls for about 15 days of releases per year: one day each in Feb. and March, 2 weekend releases in April, 2 weekends in May, 1 weekend in June, and one day each in September, October, and November. Check the American Whitewater website to find out the latest on the schedules.

Shuttle: From the Texaco/Subway in Robbinsville, drive about 17.5 miles north on US 129 to the designated paddler take out at Calderwood Lake. Backtrack about 7.5 miles south on 129 to a right turn to the dam. Follow the signs to the boater put in parking area near the dam.

52 · SLICKROCK CREEK ·

DIFFICULTY	IV (V)
LENGTH	5.5 miles
PUT-IN	Big Fat Gap Trail
TAKE-OUT	Calderwood Reservoir
ELEVATION	2011 to 1086
GRADIENT	182, 154, 157, 150, 196, 86
DRAINAGE	8.6 sq. mi.
GAUGE	visual
LEVELS	

BETA

wildcat falls - paddler jason mcclure

Slickrock Creek provides a little run adventure through one of the most beautiful wildernesses in the Southeast. Hiking into Joyce Kilmer Wilderness over a ridge on the Big Fat Gap Trail from the Cheoah valley, paddlers will put in and run 5.5 miles of class V, punctuated by the larger drops of Wildcat and Lower Falls. Wildcat Falls, which comes early in the run, is a multi-tiered drop which winds through a couple of bends. There is room to eddy between most of the drops, but the full sequence should be carefully scouted before entering. Look for a horizon line on a bend to the left, and get out river left at the lip to scout. .

Below Wildcat, the meat of the gorge begins, with quite a few technical rapids and some wood to look out for. The second large drop, Lower Falls, occurs about a mile before the lake. This river wide 12-15 footer offers several potential lines, and can be scouted or walked on the left. After the final mile, dump into Calderwood Lake and paddle out of the cove and to the right 1.75 miles to the Cheoah take out.

Overall, Slickrock Creek is more about the wilderness experience and the two bigger drops than it is about quality paddling. Most of the rest of the creek is more of a struggle than a real whitewater fun ride. Make sure you allow a lot of time for this run, since the hike in, long creek, and lake paddle make this a big day.

Shuttle: From the Texaco/Subway in Robbinsville, drive about 17.5 miles north on US 129 to the designated paddler take out at Calderwood Lake. Backtrack about 1.75 miles south on 129 to a right turn over the Cheoah. Drive across the river and make a right at the first split. Follow the signs from here to the Big Fat Gap Trailhead.

53 · CITICO CREEK ·

DIFFICULTY	III/IV
LENGTH	3.9 miles
PUT-IN	Top of road
TAKE-OUT	Junction
ELEVATION	1658 to 1215
GRADIENT	123,151,83,86
DRAINAGE	17.9 sq. mi.
GAUGE	Tellico R. at Tellico Plains (USGS) / 1-900-288-8732
LEVELS	1000+ cfs / 3.5+

BETA

📷 *mark neisler in the first rapid - photo thomas o'keefe*

This little cousin of the Tellico is a great step up from the Middle, offering a similar beautiful setting, roadside access, and fast moving class III and IV rapids. The crux of the run is Pigs in Space—a long class IV rapid that is signaled by a rock retaining wall where the road rises away from the river. This drop warrants a scout if you didn't get a look on the drive up. Below here, the river will pass through the short take out at the bridge at Doublecamp Creek Campground. If you continue downstream, be aware that there is a low head dam not far below the campground—just after a 4 foot ledge. The normal take out is 2 bridges below the dam.

Shuttle: From Tellico Plains, drive up the Tellico about 4.5 miles on 165 to a left turn near the Oosterneck parking area. Make the left, and follow this road 9 miles to a left turn at the base of the Cherohala Skyway. Follow this road about 1.25 miles to a right turn that will drop you to the Citico Creek put in. To reach the take out, continue downstream as to the bridge at the Doublecamp Campground or beyond for the longer run.

📷 *pigs in space - paddler helge klockow - photo thomas o'keefe*

📷 baby falls - paddler brian jones - photo matthew havice

📷 diaper wiper - paddler jennifer mcdonald - photo bryce yarbrough

The ledges section of the Tellico is one of the most paddled class IV creeks in the world—with big easy vertical ledges that provide loads of fun for intermediate creek boaters without tremendous difficulty or danger. The run is roadside, has excellent scenery, runs often, and provides a quick thrill that can be had several times in a day.

The run begins with some river wide vertical ledges, building in height until you reach the main attraction—12 foot Baby Falls. This drop has great lines on left and right, and lands in a deep pool. Just

below Baby Falls, the Tellico changes in character—becoming a more technical creek with some longer rapids and moves to be made. The first drop below the falls—Diaper Wiper, warrants a scout before taking the plunge at the falls. This section's finale is Jarod's Knee, a very long class IV rapid just before the take out bridge. There is some pin potential in the largest ledge of this rapid, so scout here as well.

About half way down the run the Bald River flows in from the left—dropping over the massive precipice of Bald River Falls.

Although the drop has seen one top to bottom run, the usual park 'n huck option is to carry up and run the bottom tier of the falls on the left.

Shuttle: From Tellico Plains, drive 10 miles upriver on TN 165 and park on the left just across the bridge over the Tellico for the take out. To reach the put in, drive another 2 miles upstream and pull out on the right shortly after crossing another bridge over the river.

54 · TELLICO LEDGES

DIFFICULTY	IV
LENGTH	2 miles
PUT-IN	bridge upstream of Bald River
TAKE-OUT	bridge downstream of Bald River
ELEVATION	1489 to 1282
GRADIENT	131,76
DRAINAGE	50.8 sq. mi.
GAUGE	Tellico River at Tellico Plains (TVA)
LEVELS	250+

BETA

jarod's knee - paddlers kevin colburn, sutton bacon, chris gorman - © rob maxwell   bald river falls - paddler rush peace - photo julie keller

📷 *paddler mark andes - davis kessman photo*

📷 *paddler courtney nipper - jimmy nipper photo*

The Middle Tellico is an excellent run, providing the intermediate paddler with a class III way to experience the beauty of the Tellico Gorge without the added stress of the large ledges on the section above. It also makes a great alternative for more advanced paddlers when the level is a bit on the high side for the Ledges. The entire run is roadside, allowing paddlers to bite off as much or as little as they want depending on how much time they have for their run. The run is class II with lots of class III rapids interspersed, with the class III being more frequent earlier in the run and spreading out as you get lower down. Things move pretty quickly on this run, leaving time for a second run if you want to make a full day of your trip to the Tellico.

Shuttle: From Tellico Plains, drive a little over 4.5 miles upriver (East) on TN 165 to the Oosterneck Parking area. You can take out here or at any of the pullouts upstream depending on how far you want to paddle. To reach the put in, continue upriver and park on the left just across the next bridge over the Tellico, where the road crosses to river left.

BETA

DIFFICULTY	III+
LENGTH	5.2 miles
PUT-IN	Bridge Below Bald River
TAKE-OUT	Oosterneck Rec. Area
ELEVATION	1270 to 1009
GRADIENT	50 fpm
DRAINAGE	73.6 sq. mi.
GAUGE	Tellico River at Tellico Plains (USGS) / 1-900-288-8732
LEVELS	250-2000 cfs / 1.6 - 4 ft.

WAVE SPORT

Connecting you to the liquid realm.

Robert Peerson running Hammer Factor in a Diesel, Green River Narrows   Photo: Jimi Blakeney   www.wavesport.com / www.doubleyouess.com

Ocoee - Hiwassee Region

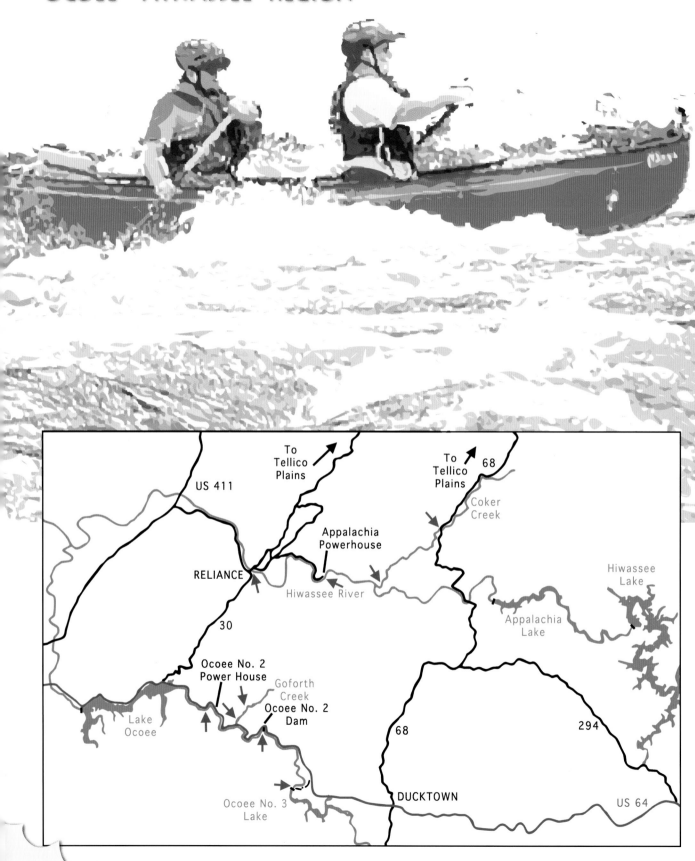

To Tellico Plains

To Tellico Plains

68

US 411

Coker Creek

Appalachia Powerhouse

RELIANCE

Hiwassee River

Hiwassee Lake

30

Appalachia Lake

Ocoee No. 2 Power House

Goforth Creek

Ocoee No. 2 Dam

Lake Ocoee

68

294

DUCKTOWN

US 64

Ocoee No. 3 Lake

56 · COKER CREEK ·

hidden abashment - paddler chris young

john lord finishes the snakedance - ben hayes photo

Coker Creek is said to have derived its name from a Cherokee woman named Coco Betsey or Coker Bess. She is listed in the official census of the Cherokee Nation conducted in 1835 as living on Coco Creek. Coco or 'Kuku' in the Cherokee language refers to the Butterfly Weed or Pleurisy Root (Asclepias tuberosa), which was often used by the Native Americans for medicinal purposes. Coker Creek is a tributary of Tennessee's Hiwassee River and offers the steep creeker plenty of excitement as well as scenic surroundings on the southern slopes of Duckett Ridge in the Unicoi Mountains.

It's a short paddle from the put-in at the USFS Coker Creek Trailhead parking area to Coker Creek Falls. Here a vertical ledge of five feet feeds directly into a steep fifteen foot slide. From here a series of broken ledges pitches down to a final river-left plummet of ten feet. This one hundred yard long section can be scouted by walking down the trail before putting on.

After the falls a short pool and good rapid leads one to the brink of the next noteworthy drop. Here the creek punches through a notch then fans out to plunge eight feet into the froth before racing over another four foot ledge. Scout on the left.

A short paddle across another pool brings one to a river-right vertical drop known to some as "Hidden Abashment." When running this drop at medium levels it's probable that one will encounter the solid rock bottom to some degree. A left line through the rhododendron is also possible. Scout on the right.

It's possible to eddy hop down to just above the next rapid (don't miss this last eddy!) where a river-right scout is in order. This is "Snakedance" and is the most technically demanding rapid on Coker Creek. It begins with a small drop onto a rock shelf then races downstream where a difficult turn in front of a large undercut boulder is required. A ride down a twisting channel finishes up one of the fastest rapids around!

From here the 2 miles to the John Muir Trail Footbridge take-out becomes a busy Class II-III run, and is generally boat-scoutable. Always be on the lookout for wood on this run.

Multiple runs from the top down to Snakedance are possible (hike back up the trail on river-right) as well as combining this run with the Citico or Tellico in the same day. Coker Creek is usually runable when

DIFFICULTY	IV (V)
LENGTH	5.2 miles
PUT-IN	TN 68 bridge
TAKE-OUT	Muir Trail
ELEVATION	1461 to 961
GRADIENT	37,24,153,152,119,15
DRAINAGE	19.3 sq. mi.
GAUGE	68 bridge gauge
LEVELS	0 to 6" (cl IV)

BETA

the Tellico is 3.5 or higher, and is a notch up in difficulty from the Tellico Ledges.

Ken Strickland

Shuttle: On the north side of the Highway 68/Coker Creek Bridge, turn and travel 0.7 on county #625 to the top of the hill where you will intersect county #626 (Duckett Ridge Rd). Take a left for 2.3 miles to where USFS 2138 enters on the left. Turn here and travel a mile down to the dead end at the creek (put-in). To get to the take-out, travel back up USFS 2138 to its junction with Duckett Ridge Rd. Take a left for 3.1 miles until the road dead ends at the John Muir Trail crossing.

DIFFICULTY	I/II
LENGTH	5.85 miles
PUT-IN	Appalachia Powerhouse
TAKE-OUT	Reliance
ELEVATION	839 to 738
GRADIENT	17 fpm
DRAINAGE	Every Day Memorial Day - Labor day, Saturdays Sept. & Oct., & random
GAUGE	1-800-238-2264-4-22-#
LEVELS	1-2 Generators

BETA

📷 © LD

The Hiwassee is a fantastic class I/II river offering a multitude of braided channels, rapids, put ins, take outs, small surf waves, and island lunch spots sure to provide the perfect day on the water for any paddler. Make sure you bring your sunscreen and your cash—every parking spot on this river requires a small fee, and the wide open river channel provides an excellent breeding ground for melanoma. The wide channel leaves plenty of room for the ample crowds that frequent this run on summer weekends. Also remember to steer clear of the many fishermen using this river—unless you want to bring your rod and join right in.

Shuttle: From the Ocoee, drive west on 64 to a right turn on TN 30 near Ocoee Lake. Follow TN 30 about 8.75 miles to the town of Reliance, where you can leave a take out vehicle. Cross the Hiwassee and make the first right. Go about 1.25 miles, and make another right, driving over the hill and dropping down to the river. Drive up the river and choose a put in anywhere between here and Appalachia Powerhouse.

📷 lunch break - © LD

© LD

DIFFICULTY	III/IV
LENGTH	5 miles
PUT-IN	Ocoee #3 Dam
TAKE-OUT	Ocoee #2 Dam
ELEVATION	1350 to 1109
GRADIENT	48 fmp
SEASON	Weekends April - October, 8:30 - 4:30
GAUGE	http://www.tva.com/
LEVELS	river/recreation/ocoeesched.htm

Formerly a high water only treat, the Upper Ocoee has become a staple from late spring through early fall over the last few years. Dewatered by the TVA since the early 20th century, the river received some major renovations in preparation for the 1996 Olympic Slalom competition. Now the Olympic Section offers some great rapids and playspots, and the rest of the river has regular releases on weekends in April - September as well. Some paddlers choose to just run the Olympic Section, or to paddle from the #3 dam to the bottom of the Olympic Stretch, while others enjoy the longer trip putting in at the #3 dam and paddling down to dam #2. Since the Middle Ocoee runs on every day that the Upper does, a full day can be made of combining the two sections.

Putting in at the #3 dam, you will wind your way through a plant cluttered class II riverbed for about a mile before the pace picks up with several class III rapids. Upon entering the Olympic Course, the river will narrow down into the channel built for the Olympics, and the river will consequently increase tremendously in power. The main obstacle to be aware of in this stretch is Humongous, a huge hole located about 3/4 of the way down the Olympic Section on river right.

Below the Olympic Section, there is one more rapid of note— Roach Motel—and then some runout to the lake. Beware of a low head dam style ledge right before the lake, just after passing under the bridge to the Thunder Rock Campground. This drop, known as Edge of the World, can be run in several places with caution, or it can be skirted far river right.

Shuttle: Take US 64 west from NC or east from Cleveland, TN to the Ocoee River near Ducktown. Leave your take out vehicle either at the parking area at Ocoee Dam No. 2 (obvious 30 ft. dam) for a long run, or at the bottom of the Olympic Course ($3 parking fee) for a shorter run. Drive east from the Olympic Visitor's Center a little over 1.5 miles to a right turn, and proceed to the parking area near the dam.

© LD

59 · CALLAHAN'S LEDGES ·

Callahan's Ledges is a great park and play spot on the Olympic Whitewater Course on the Upper Ocoee. Located about 2/3 of the way down the run on river left, this spot offers up nice wheels, right blunts, and other fun with excellent eddy service. Be aware that if you exit the surfer's left side of the wave, the giant hole at Humongous is shortly downstream. Several other fun spots make it worthwhile to paddle the whole Olympic Section and walk your shuttle to get in a little more play.

Directions: Drive east from Cleveland, TN or west from Murphy, NC to the Olympic Visitor's Center in the Ocoee Gorge. Callahan's Ledges is about 2/3 of the way down the Olympic Section on river left.

Gage and Levels: The Upper Ocoee runs most Saturdays and Sundays from late April through mid October. Releases are from 8:30 - 4:30, meaning you can surf from about 10 - 5.

© LD

60 · GOFORTH CREEK ·

BETA

DIFFICULTY	V
LENGTH	.3 miles
PUT-IN	Hike
TAKE-OUT	Goforth Confluence
ELEVATION	1122 to 958
GRADIENT	164
DRAINAGE	4 sq. mi.
GAUGE	visual
LEVELS	

Hidden right under the noses of almost every paddler in the Southeast lies one of the most beautiful high quality creek runs in the country. Goforth creek drops 165 ft. in .3 miles before running under Hwy 64 into the Ocoee. The last rapid looks ugly from the road, but the hidden river right channel provides an excellent route around this log choked splatterfest. Your best bet for success here is to scout the entire run with no water. Bring a picnic, a foam boater or a pretty lady up the creek for a delightful break from the hubbub of the Ocoee.

The rapids have great personality—screaming fast slides, 8' boofs, and super-technical rock dodges. Look for black clouds and heavy rain up the valley, then wait about forty minutes for the creek to rise. A very heavy rain will run Goforth for up to 20 hours. Beware putting in on rising water, as Goforth can get surly. Also check very carefully for wood—it's a tiny creek. Walk up the river right trail and put in where it gets flat. Round trip takes about ten minutes if you boogie. Have fun!

Shuttle: Pull off of US 64 at Goforth Creek, 2.3 miles west of Ocoee #2 Dam and 1.9 miles east of the #2 powerhouse at Hell Hole.

Chris Harjes

📷 *paddler todd grafe - © rob maxwell*

141

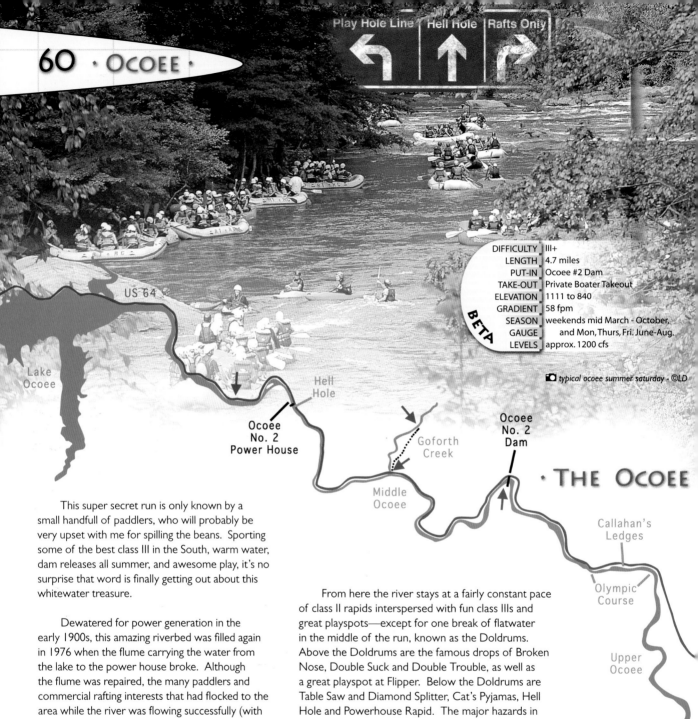

60 · OCOEE

Play Hole Line ← | Hell Hole ↑ | Rafts Only →

US 64

Lake Ocoee

Ocoee No. 2 Power House

Hell Hole

Goforth Creek

Middle Ocoee

Ocoee No. 2 Dam

BETA

DIFFICULTY	III+
LENGTH	4.7 miles
PUT-IN	Ocoee #2 Dam
TAKE-OUT	Private Boater Takeout
ELEVATION	1111 to 840
GRADIENT	58 fpm
SEASON	weekends mid March - October,
GAUGE	and Mon, Thurs, Fri. June-Aug.
LEVELS	approx. 1200 cfs

📷 *typical ocoee summer saturday - ©LD*

· THE OCOEE

Callahan's Ledges

Olympic Course

Upper Ocoee

Ocoee No. 3 Lake

This super secret run is only known by a small handfull of paddlers, who will probably be very upset with me for spilling the beans. Sporting some of the best class III in the South, warm water, dam releases all summer, and awesome play, it's no surprise that word is finally getting out about this whitewater treasure.

Dewatered for power generation in the early 1900s, this amazing riverbed was filled again in 1976 when the flume carrying the water from the lake to the power house broke. Although the flume was repaired, the many paddlers and commercial rafting interests that had flocked to the area while the river was flowing successfully (with a struggle) attained regular releases from the TVA. Those releases continue today, providing water for more paddlers than travel any other river in the Southeast.

Walking down the crowded boat ramp at the #2 dam, paddlers are immediately faced with the most difficult move of the day—successfully making it to river left in the first rapid to avoid the hole at Grumpy's Ledge. If you make this class III move, you're probably going to be fine on the Ocoee. If the move looks too hairy for you, walk down the road and put in below the hole.

From here the river stays at a fairly constant pace of class II rapids interspersed with fun class IIIs and great playspots—except for one break of flatwater in the middle of the run, known as the Doldrums. Above the Doldrums are the famous drops of Broken Nose, Double Suck and Double Trouble, as well as a great playspot at Flipper. Below the Doldrums are Table Saw and Diamond Splitter, Cat's Pyjamas, Hell Hole and Powerhouse Rapid. The major hazards in all of these rapids—as well as all the smaller rapids in between—are rafts, which you will find in plenty on the Ocoee. Despite the crowds, rafts, and the urban roadside feel of the river, there are few better places to be on a hot summer weekend than surfing it up on the Ocoee.

Shuttle: The take out is the private boater parking area on US 64, a little over 5 miles west of Ocoee #2 Dam and 2.5 - 3 miles east of the US 64 / TN 30 junction near Ocoee Lake. To reach the put in, drive just over 5 miles east to the parking area at Ocoee #2 Dam.

📷 *taft sibley skirting grumpy's ledge - ©LD*

📷 *brian madsen goes for the hairy ferry at double suck - ©LD*

📷 *double trouble - guide andria baldovin - ©LD*

61 · HELL HOLE ·

top wave - paddler chris stafford - ©LD

paddler chris stafford - photo chris young

Hell Hole is the classic southeastern play spot and has been home to numerous rodeo competitions, including the 1993 World Championships. The feature consists of a very fast wave just upstream of the main attraction—a fluffy hole with a nice pile, good shoulders, and a deep pocket. The riverbed is quite loose here, so the hole changes over time as rocks shift and local experts fine tune the spot. Almost all the time, Hell Hole offers everything from a friendly first experience with a big hole to ends, blunts, and aerial loops. Some parking is available along the roadside across the river from the Ocoee #2 Power Plant, but be respectful of the no-parking areas and make sure your car is well off the road.

When to go: Hell Hole runs any time there is a release on the Middle Ocoee. The river runs Saturdays and Sundays from mid-March through mid-October. Between Labor day and Memorial Day, it also runs on Mondays, Thursdays, and Fridays.

Shuttle: Pull off US 64 near the Ocoee # 2 Powerhouse, 4.25 miles west of Ocoee #2 Dam and a little over 3.5 miles east of the 64/TN 30 junction near Ocoee Lake.

paddler shanna powell - © LD

THE SMOKIES

GREAT SMOKY
MOUNTAINS
NATIONAL PARK
AN INTERNATIONAL BIOSPHERE RESERVE

lower big creek - paddler john pilson - ©LD

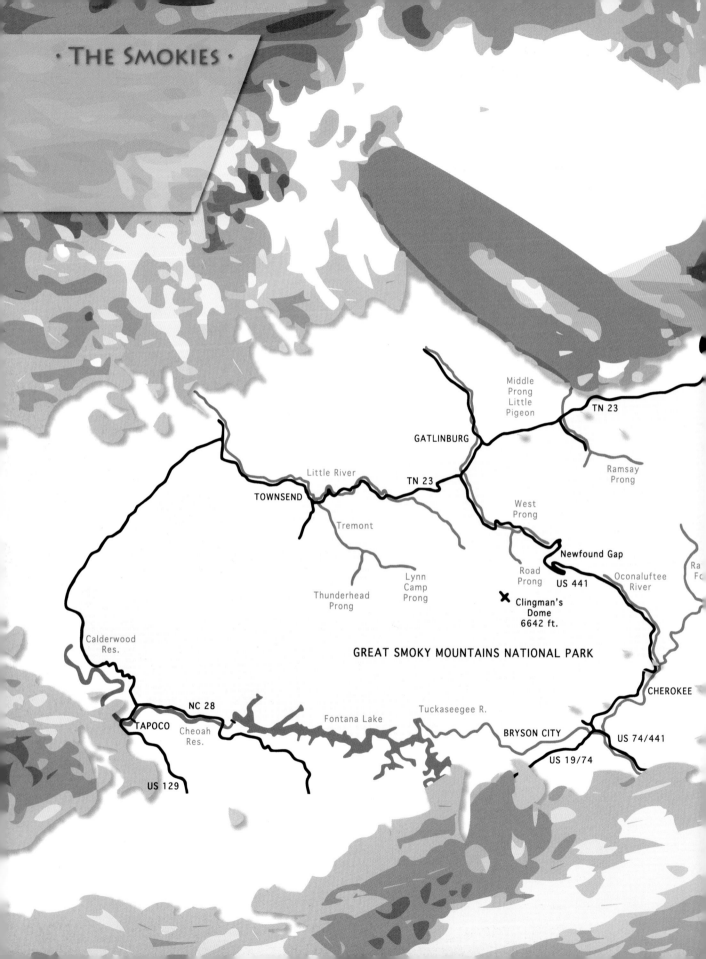

· THE SMOKIES ·

Middle Prong Little Pigeon

TN 23

GATLINBURG

Little River

TN 23

Ramsay Prong

TOWNSEND

West Prong

Tremont

Newfound Gap

Lynn Camp Prong

Road Prong

US 441

Oconaluftee River

Ra Fo

Thunderhead Prong

✗ Clingman's Dome 6642 ft.

Calderwood Res.

GREAT SMOKY MOUNTAINS NATIONAL PARK

CHEROKEE

NC 28

Tuckaseegee R.

TAPOCO

Fontana Lake

BRYSON CITY

US 74/441

Cheoah Res.

US 19/74

US 129

HARTFORD

Pigeon
River

Big
Creek

I-40

Waterville
Lake

Cataloochee
Creek

WAYNES-
VILLE

Jonathan
Creek

ELK
XING

63 · LITTLE RIVER ·

remember - no break dancing down waterfalls

the author runs the sinks - andria baldovin photo

The Little River from the Sinks to the Elbow is the classic Smokies run, and has been offering a great roadside class III/IV experience to paddlers for decades. Although many sections of this river can be run, this most popular section contains the most difficult whitewater, and is the most used. The Little can provide anything from fun technical creeking to pushy powerful big water depending on the levels, and the scenery is excellent in this corner of the National Park.

Pulling into the Sinks parking lot, the largest drop on the run—the Sinks—will be quite obvious. Crossing the road and looking upstream, you will see several more lead in ledges ending in a hole with pin rocks lurking on the left. You can carry up and run the intro, put in just upstream of the bridge to run the big drop, or carry down the left bank to put in below. The Sinks offers a few lines—the most common two being a right to left slide or the vertical drop into a hole on river left.

BETA		
DIFFICULTY	III (IV x 2)
LENGTH	3 miles
PUT-IN	The Sinks
TAKE-OUT	The Elbow
ELEVATION	1574 to 1259
GRADIENT	128, 95, 92
DRAINAGE	53.1 sq. mi.
GAUGE	Little R. near Townsend (visual or boatingbeta.com) / Little R. at Maryville
LEVELS	2.5' - 4.5' / 600+ cfs

andria baldovin at the elbow - ©LD

andria baldovin at the sinks - ©LD

Heading downstream, paddlers will be greeted with a large number of fun class III drops, with one larger drop occurring just upstream of where a tributary drops over a 15 foot waterfall and into the river on the side opposite the road (visible from the shuttle). Below this, things will mellow until a final flurry of class III+ before the last big drop—the Elbow. The Elbow is on the easier end of class IV, but beware of the undercut lurking at the bottom right—it will not be fatal, but could certainly be inconvenient. Most folks park at the paved pullout 100 yards below the Elbow, but it is also possible to continue another 3 miles down to the Y.

Gauge: The gauge is found about 1/4 mile downstream of the confluence with the Middle Prong at the Y.

Shuttle: From Townsend, drive east on 73 a little over 5 miles to the pullout 100 yards before the Elbow. To reach the put in, continue on 73 2.9 miles to the second bridge upstream at the Sinks, and put in a short distance upstream of the bridge.

lead in to the sinks - jennifer petosa photo

64 · LYNN CAMP PRONG ·

Lynn Camp Prong is a beautiful continuous Smokies micro creek, with non stop class III/IV action broken only by one gigantic manky monstrosity of a class V+ waterfall known as Kick Yer Dog Falls. Kick Yer Dog is clearly visible from the trail on the way up. Most paddlers will want to put in below the falls and run down as an exciting lead-in to a Tremont Run. More adventurous souls can pick their lines and roll the dice on the falls and the lead in drops—which are considerable. The pace mellows below the falls until it picks up for one final thrill just above the bridge at the confluence with the Thunderhead Prong.

Shuttle: From Townsend, head east on 73 for a little over 2 miles to a right at the junction. Shortly after, you will cross the Middle Prong of the Little and make a left up the river. Continue to the trailhead all the way at the end of the road. Park here and hike across the bridge and upstream as far as you like to put in on the Lynn Camp Prong.

📷 *paddler andria baldovin - ©LD*

DIFFICULTY	III/IV (V+)
LENGTH	3.15 miles
PUT-IN	Hike up
TAKE-OUT	Confluence with thunderhead prong
ELEVATION	2828 to 1900
GRADIENT	280,274,330,44
DRAINAGE	5.6 sq. mi.
GAUGE	Visual
LEVELS	

BETA

📷 byron sambat boofs as daniel sanders looks on - ©LD

DIFFICULTY	III/IV
LENGTH	3 miles
PUT-IN	Lynn Camp / Thunderhead confl.
TAKE-OUT	Tremont Institute
ELEVATION	1880 to 1354
GRADIENT	200, 185, 141
DRAINAGE	21.1 sq. mi.
GAUGE	Little River at Townsend
LEVELS	

BETA

The Tremont run on the Middle Prong of the Little River is a super fun class III/IV- introduction to creeking. It has the continuous nature typical of Smokies Runs, and down scaled versions of many of the challenges you will find on other creeks as well: wood, smaller eddies, small slots, and numerous small boofs. It is the perfect training ground for paddlers looking to learn the skills necessary to step up to runs like the Middle Prong of the Little Pigeon, or some of the sections of Big Creek. For class III boaters looking for a little thrill, this run provides roadside ease of access and classically beautiful Smokies scenery.

The largest rapid on the run is found adjacent to a stop sign that is randomly placed along the road. This ledge can develop pretty large holes at higher levels, so a scout on the way up might be advised. Most of the rest of the run is easily visible from the road—which also offers the flexibility of putting in and taking out where ever you like. No matter how much of this run you hit, the super fun rapids and incredible scenery are bound to bring you back for many more runs!

Shuttle: From Townsend, head east on 73 for a little over 2 miles to a right at the junction. Shortly after, you will cross the Middle Prong of the Little and make a left up the river. Continue to the trailhead all the way at the end of the road for the put in. A variety of takeouts are available downstream of here, with the most common being pullouts near the Tremont Institute.

📷 andria at the biggest drop - ©LD

66 · ALUM CAVE ·

DIFFICULTY	V+
LENGTH	1.7 miles
PUT-IN	Chimneytops Trailhead
TAKE-OUT	Chimneys Picnic Area
ELEVATION	3419 to 2535
GRADIENT	365, 319
DRAINAGE	12.6 sq. mi.
GAUGE	Chimneys Picnic Area Bridge/Newfound Gap Rain Gauge
LEVELS	

BETA

📷 *dooley tombras headed downstream*

The Alum Cave section of the Walker Camp Prong is the run of choice for those who head to the West Prong and find it too high—if you aren't ready for the turbo-hair to be found on the Road Prong. With slightly less gradient and difficulty than the Lower West Prong for most of its length, and a super tight streambed with continuous rapids, Alum Cave is a high speed high elevation conveyor belt of fun.

Putting in at the Alum Cave trailhead, the whitewater will be moderate for the first mile. Keep a close eye out for wood, though, because it tends to accumulate in some of the bends on this run. When you pass under a bridge and 441 goes from river left to river right, get ready for action. The pace builds to class V for a ways from here to the take out at the foot bridge at the Chimneytops Trailhead. If you're not up for the added challenge, you can take out on river right just below the bridge.

Shuttle: The put in is at the Alum Cave trailhead parking area on US 441, 4.3 miles north of Newfound Gap and 8.6 miles south of the Sugarlands Visitor's Center. The take out is 1.7 miles north at the Chimney Tops trailhead parking area.

📷 *dumpin' time*

Sugarlands Visitors' Center

Gatlinburg

Maryville

4th Quiet Walkway

Cambell Overlook Takeout

West Prong Little Pigeon

Lower West Prong

· WEST PRONG LITTLE PIGEON ·

Chimneytops Trailhead

Trailhead Section

Alum Cave Trailhead

Chimneys Picnic Area

Alum Cave Section

Road Prong

Newfound Gap

Cherokee

Clingman's Dome

Background: headed into room without a view - lower west prong

67 · ROAD PRONG ·

The Road Prong is one of the steepest, hardest creeks in the area—and is a great high water alternative to the West Prong if you're up for a thrill. This run drains a ridge off the second highest peak in the East—6642 ft. Clingman's Dome—and wastes no time in making its way down the hill. It offers a hike in from the Clingman's Dome Road to the steep upper mile, or a hike up from the Chimneytops Trailhead to run the slightly less steep lower mile.

This creek is characterized by non-stop action—with a couple of bigger rapids in the upper section that will make all but the gnarliest paddlers cry for Mommy. The lower section maintains the speed—screaming around corners and over blind drops with few eddies, and plenty of wood and other obstacles to avoid. If you're used to micro creeking in Colorado this run will only be a small step up—if not, expect to be scared out of your head more than once.

Upon reaching the confluence with the West Prong, you can continue down for a high water run on the upper if you have death wish or a reservoir of adrenaline remaining.

Shuttle: The takeout for the Road Prong is at the Chimneytops trailhead on 441, 6 miles north of Newfound Gap and 6.9 miles south of the Sugarlands Visitors' Center. You can either carry up the trail as far along the Road Prong as you want to go, or you can hike in from the top by driving just past Newfound Gap and taking the road to Clingman's Dome on the right. Hike the trail that splits off to the right just over a mile out this road.

amos shuman - john parch photo

amos shuman boofin' the road prong - john parch photo

DIFFICULTY	V+
LENGTH	1.9 miles
PUT-IN	Clingman's Dome Road
TAKE-OUT	Chimneytops Trailhead
ELEVATION	4451 to 3359
GRADIENT	616, 476
DRAINAGE	2 sq. mi.
GAUGE	Chimneys Picnic Area Bridge / Visual Gage and Gps
LEVELS	2'+ / 2"+ in 6 hours

BETA

trip kinney, amos shuman, mefford williams, and jeb hall headed downstream - john parch photo

68 · UPPER WEST PRONG - THE TRAILHEAD ·

Once you feel like you have mastered the West Prong from Picnic area down, the next step is to add the 1.7 miles from the Chimney Tops trail head to the picnic area. Except for a 1/4 mile section, it is no harder than the Lower West Prong.

Most park and put in at the Chimney trail head parking lot and follow the trail down to the wooden bridge to start. At levels above 1.1 ft, you can add 250 yards of good whitewater by parking at the overflow parking upstream and walking to the river at the start of the hwy 441 loop (see Alum Cave section).

The first 4/5 of a mile is about as hard as what one can see from the trailhead bridge. Continuous fairly safe small rounded boulder drops are the rule. Moving pools are the exception. At the end of this section you will find one of these exceptions. From this pool you can look down a long straight section of river which starts to increase in difficultly. This "Straightaway" leads into the hard section. "Freeze Frame" has been changing over the past two years. The 7' boof off the center is losing its water as the left channel deepens. After a 4' river wide ledge with a hole on the left is a small pool above "Dinosaur". Three drops lead into the main drop. **WARNING**: Boats tend to get pushed into a swirling eddy/hole at the bottom left of the drop. A lot of water and a few kayaks go in the undercut beneath the big rocks. Following a boof with a narrow landing, you will hopefully notice a metal box in the river on the left. Sneak the top of "Metal Box" on the left through a 6' spout to avoid the main channel, which contains

undercuts and wood. The last big rapid—"Big Tree"—comes below. Usually a three drop rapid on the right, at this time the 2nd drop has a big tree in it making it unrunable. A scrapey sneak is available on the left.

After the big stuff, UWP starts to ease up. Once you see picnic tables or smell the burgers cooking, the takeout at the hwy 441 bridge is 1/4 mile away. Do not wave at the spectators too much—this picnic section has eaten many boaters who thought they were done.

The Gauge on the downstream left side of the hwy 441 bridge changes every couple of years. As of winter 2004, the range of runable level is from .7' to 1.6'. From .7'-.9' I usually put-in 1/4 mile downstream of the 441 tunnel at the big pull off and look for the unmarked trail on the upstream side. I also park my car at the furthest point upstream at the picnic take out. Be careful from 1.22-1.6' as this is the high end.

If you run into trouble along the way, hike out river right from put in to Dinosaur. Below Dinosaur, follow the deer trail downstream on river left.

Howard Tidwell

Shuttle: The git-in for the upper west prong is at the Chimneytops Trailhead on 441, 6 miles north of Newfound Gap and 6.9 miles south of the Sugarlands Visitors' Center. Take out about 2.5 miles down the road at the Chimneys Picnic Area.

DIFFICULTY	V
LENGTH	3.4 miles
PUT-IN	Chimneys Picnic Area
TAKE-OUT	Lower Quiet Walkway
ELEVATION	2736 to 1639
GRADIENT	321, 349, 338, 89
DRAINAGE	14.4 sq. mi.
GAUGE	Chimneys Picnic Area Bridge/Newfound Gap Rain Gauge
LEVELS	2"+ in 12 hours

BETA

paddler nate helms - toby mcdermott photo (top)
paddler chris young - ©LD (left)
paddler scott harkey - ©LD (center)
glen laplante, adam hertzog, and scott harkey
- ©LD (right)

69 · LOWER WEST PRONG ·

The Lower West Prong is one of the finest stretches of whitewater anywhere on Earth, with crystal clear water, incredible scenery, and relentless gradient that just keeps steadily falling at over 300 feet per mile, with no drops larger than 10 feet and no real pools to speak of. The river has a somewhat western style due to the continuity, but the tight slots, obstructed riverbed, and plentiful—if small—eddies make this the perfect combination of the best of both worlds.

Putting in at the picnic area, paddlers will have little time to warm up—you put into a riverbed that is much like it will be for the next several miles, absolutely continuous. Things ease up for a while a few hundred yards down from the bridge, but after paddling to the left of the first island the breaks will pretty much be over for good. As you continue down the run, the continuous class IV/V will be littered with places where the difficulty and gradient pick up to class V, and these class Vs will become bigger and more frequent as the run progresses.

The height of the fun occurs a little over 2 miles into the run, with the biggest drops of Amtrak and Room Without a View occurring within about 1/4 mile of one another. Amtrak has a long lead in and tends to sneak up on unwary paddlers, but can be spotted by looking for a large boulder sticking up on river left at a horizon line after a long class II/III lead-in. Room Without a View is not far downstream, but has good eddies at the lip, and is scoutable from river right.

It's not over after the big two—several more class V drops remain before the lower take out at the final quiet walkway. The Campbell Overlook take out is found about three good sized rapids below Room, after a pinny rock bashy rapid which starts from an eddy on the right and ends in an eddy on the left. Get out on the left, and carry upstream about 100 yards until you see another trail branch sharply off to the right up the hill.

The final class V at the bottom—In a Hurry—sneaks up on you well after the rapids have eased up. It's found in a bend to the right with some wood and other nasties on the outside of the bend. If you plan to continue below the Campbell Overlook on your run, either take a good guide or be very wary for that last burst of class V at the bottom.

With only a couple of exceptions, the continuous nature of this creek causes most of the class Vs to have lengthy lead ins with few eddies—leading to inadvertent and uncontrolled runs for those who don't know the river well. A good guide is highly recommended for this run—and will speed up the process enough that you'll have time to make it back up for a second lap before dark.

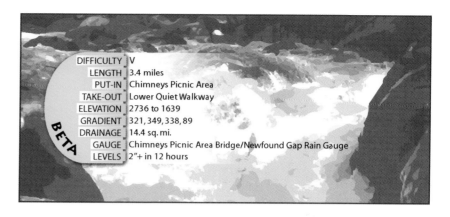

BETA	
DIFFICULTY	V
LENGTH	3.4 miles
PUT-IN	Chimneys Picnic Area
TAKE-OUT	Lower Quiet Walkway
ELEVATION	2736 to 1639
GRADIENT	321, 349, 338, 89
DRAINAGE	14.4 sq. mi.
GAUGE	Chimneys Picnic Area Bridge/Newfound Gap Rain Gauge
LEVELS	2"+ in 12 hours

Gauge: The gauge on the downstream river left of the bridge near the Chimneys Picnic area is useful in a relative sense, but changes every few months with good rains. Check with the locals to get a current correlation for the gauge.

Shuttle: The git-in is at the Chimneys Picnic Area on 441, about 4.5 miles from the Sugarlands Visitor's center and 8.5 miles from Newfound Gap. You can take out either at the Campbell Overlook pullout, or at the 4th quiet walkway, which is about 3.5 miles down the road from the git-in.

buffy bailey burge driving the train at amtrak - ©LD

70 · RAMSAY PRONG ·

DIFFICULTY	IV/V
LENGTH	1.7 miles
PUT-IN	Ramsay Cascades Trailhead
TAKE-OUT	Porter's Creek
ELEVATION	2080 to 1665
GRADIENT	282, 133
DRAINAGE	18.2 sq.mi.
GAUGE	USGS L. Pigeon at Sevierville
LEVELS	2500+

BETA

The Ramsay Prong is a great Smokies run—a smaller version of Big Creek or the West Prong that is slightly more manageable for folks not accustomed to this continuous style of water. Put in for the drop just above the foot bridge—or start just below—and boof your way down to the confluence with Porter's Creek, enjoying loads of great rapids along the way. Be wary of wood on this stream, and have a look at things on the drive up—it comes at you really fast once you're on the water. The whole thing is roadside—so you can get out any time you like if the pace of the river gets ahead of you. For an added class V+ thrill, more aggressive boaters carry up and run the couple of miles above here, where the difficulty and gradient pick up considerably.

Shuttle: From Gatlinburg, head East 5.5 - 6 miles to Greenbrier Rd., just before the bridge over the Middle Prong of the Little Pigeon. Turn up Greenbrier and head upstream along the river to the takeout at the confluence with Porter's Creek. To reach the put in, turn left across Porter's Creek and continue up the road to the parking lot at the gate. You can put in here or cross the foot bridge and hike up as high as you want for some solid class V action.

inset top right - mike vanderwerf - jdy photo , inset bottom left - kevin colburn - © LD, above - philip dann - jennifer day young photo

71 · GREENBRIER ·

BETA

DIFFICULTY	III/IV
LENGTH	3 miles
PUT-IN	Porter's Creek
TAKE-OUT	US 321
ELEVATION	1657 to 1362
GRADIENT	89,119,87
DRAINAGE	37.7 sq. mi.
GAUGE	USGS Little Pigeon at Sevierville
LEVELS	2000+

Greenbrier is a fun class III/IV run through a wide valley on the edge of the National Park. This excellent intermediate run is frequently visible from the road on the drive up. Most of the large rapids are well defined, although the river gets pushy and more continuous in character at high water. Its larger riverbed and proximity to both Knoxville and the Pigeon area make this an excellent cool down run after another trip in the park or a hard day at work.

Shuttle: From Gatlinburg, head East 5.5 - 6 miles to Greenbrier Rd., just before the bridge over the Middle Prong of the Little Pigeon. Turn up Greenbrier and park for the takeout. To reach the put in, head upstream along the river to the confluence with Porter's Creek.

©LD

72 · CATALOOCHEE CREEK ·

BETA

DIFFICULTY	III
LENGTH	3.5 miles
PUT-IN	F.R. 284
TAKE-OUT	Waterville Lake
ELEVATION	2452 to 2257
GRADIENT	63,81,51
DRAINAGE	49.3 sq. mi.
GAUGE	Cataloochee Creek USGS
LEVELS	200+

Cataloochee Creek is a beautiful run, significant in that it is the only easily accessible roadless run in the park that is less than class V in difficulty. It also drains one of the most beautiful valleys in the park—a place that is home to the only herd of elk in the east—reintroduced there in the 90s.

Putting in at the campground, the whitewater will be mellow and scenic for quite a ways. In the second half of the run, there are several bigger class III rapids which are the most difficult on the creek. Below this, the creek will dump into Waterville Lake—arguably the most polluted body of water in the country. Be careful not to stir up the sediment as you paddle across and get out on the far side, walking down to the rest area and your waiting car.

Shuttle: The take out for this run is the rest area off of east bound I-40 between exits 7 and 15. To reach the put in, continue east on I-40 to exit 20. Make a right at the bottom of the ramp, and another right almost immediately. From here it is a matter of following the signs up over the mountain to the Cataloochee Valley area of the Great Smoky Mountains National Park. When you drop down and cross the creek, make a right and continue to the camp ground.

· LOWER PIGEON DRAINAGE ·

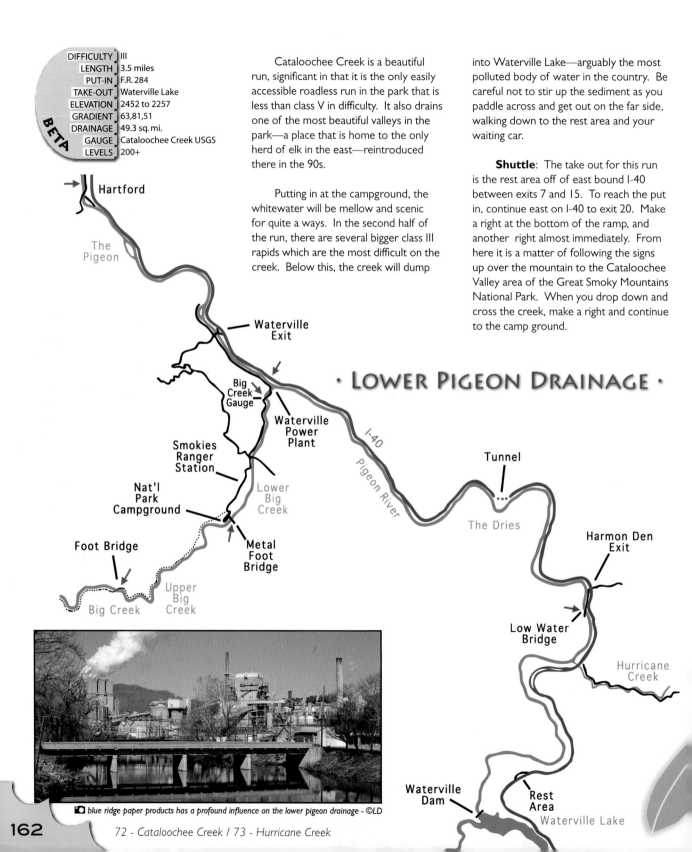

📷 *blue ridge paper products has a profound influence on the lower pigeon drainage - ©LD*

73 · HURRICANE CREEK ·

Hurricane Creek is a short little thrill that makes a great option if you arrive at Big Creek and find it too high. The creek is tiny, and probably deserves its name because it practically takes a hurricane to produce enough rain to run it. If you can catch it, however, it offers some really cool micro creeking and is probably the most beautiful creek you'll ever find within 1/2 mile of the interstate.

Make the sketchy turn from I-40 and drive up into the tiny gorge, picking a spot to put in once the creek rises up to the road. There are several class V spots on the way down, finishing with a really cool drop that leads right into a culvert under I-40. Although the culvert has been run, it's a scary proposition indeed—requiring a long dark traverse under the entire interstate and into the Dries of the Pigeon. Most folks set good safety to catch boaters and prevent them from washing into the culvert.

Shuttle: This creek can only be accessed from I-40 westbound. If you are eastbound, you will have to continue to exit 15 and turn around. Drive west on I-40 about 4 miles and pass the rest area. About 2 miles past the rest area, you will see a sign that says the Harmon Den Exit is 1 mile away. Slow down, your turn is just past that sign. Make a right turn off the interstate onto a small dirt road, and park in the pullout on the right for the take out. Drive up the dirt road as far as you like to put in.

📷 the entrace to the culvert - ©LD

📷 paddler john pilson - ©LD

DIFFICULTY	V
LENGTH	.55 miles
PUT-IN	Hurricane Creek Road
TAKE-OUT	I-40
ELEVATION	2150 to 1951
GRADIENT	199
DRAINAGE	8.4 sq. mi.
GAUGE	visual
LEVELS	

BETA

74 · PIGEON DRIES ·

DIFFICULTY	IV/V
LENGTH	7.2 miles
PUT-IN	Harmon Den
TAKE-OUT	Waterville Power Plant
ELEVATION	1857 to 1376
GRADIENT	27, 25, 67, 118, 98, 82, 35, 29
DRAINAGE	468.5 sq. mi.
GAUGE	
LEVELS	350 - 2500 cfs

BETA

nowhere to land - © rob maxwell

The Dries of the Pigeon is one of the best class IV-V river runs, depending on flow, in the southeast. However, the Pigeon River was the big loser to corporate interests that have left indelible imprints on the river and the gorge. The result is a small, ill-conceived access road (i.e. I-40) and some of the worst water quality in Western North Carolina. It is called the Dries because of the dam that leaves the run almost continuously de-watered except for after very heavy rains.

The put in is at Exit 7 on I-40, the Harmon Den exit, at the low water bridge. The upper couple of miles are flatwater with intermittent class two. The run truly starts at a long left bend in the river where you can see large amounts of road blast on the bank with the larger chunks in the river. A lengthy series of ledge holes builds gradually with most of the water ending left through some sharper rocks; watch for a piton. This sets the tone for the run.

The rapids are mostly ledge holes with tongues alternating to different sides of the river. At lower flows—under 900 cfs—there are several small boofs. At higher flows—around 1400 cfs—you've just got to fire it up and hit stuff with your head. The biggest rapids are Picket Fences (a series of large ledge holes), No Where To Land (a ten foot ledge that lands on rocks. At low water you run it on the left—at high water right off the middle or sneak it far right). The third named rapid is Chinese Arithmetic, made up of a series of sticky ledge holes with a large snaking tongue. It's a really fun rapid, except that the center of the rapid pours into a sieve. This was the site of a boater fatality in 2001 during a rare stretch when the Dries ran almost continuously for five months due to work on the surge tank at the power plant.

After this the river serves up more of the same class IV that you were running before the big ones. When you get to a large over hung canyon wall there is a great surfing wave (1100-1400 cfs). This is a great run for a playboat/river runner,

but only if you are comfortable surfing large holes you did not want to be in and can deal with being pushed towards things you don't like the looks of. Take a creek boat if this isn't you.

The last mile eases considerably to the take out just after Waterville Power Plant. We have a tradition of taking a roll or two in the crystalline waters of Big Creek and washing some of the stink from the dirty bird off. We marvel at the contrast between the rivers and the impact of humans on the land, and then we load up our trucks to do another run.

Trip Kinney & Jeb Hall

Shuttle: To reach the take out, take exit 451 from I-40 in Tennessee. Cross the river and make a left, driving upriver to Waterville Power Plant. Park here. To reach the put in, get back on I-40 heading east and go to exit 7 (Harmon Den). Make a right off the ramp and follow the road to the river. Put in below the low water bridge.

kevin thomas falls victim to tiny tower - © rob maxwell

put in bridge at 874 cfs. - © rob maxwell

75 · UPPER BIG CREEK ·

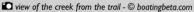

BETA		
DIFFICULTY	V
LENGTH	2.5 miles
PUT-IN	Foot Bridge
TAKE-OUT	Metal Foot Bridge
ELEVATION	2381 to 1728
GRADIENT	302, 301, 50
DRAINAGE	23.1 sq. mi.
GAUGE	SSR 1397 Bridge or Cataloochee Cr.
LEVELS	1.6 ft. + (250+ cfs)

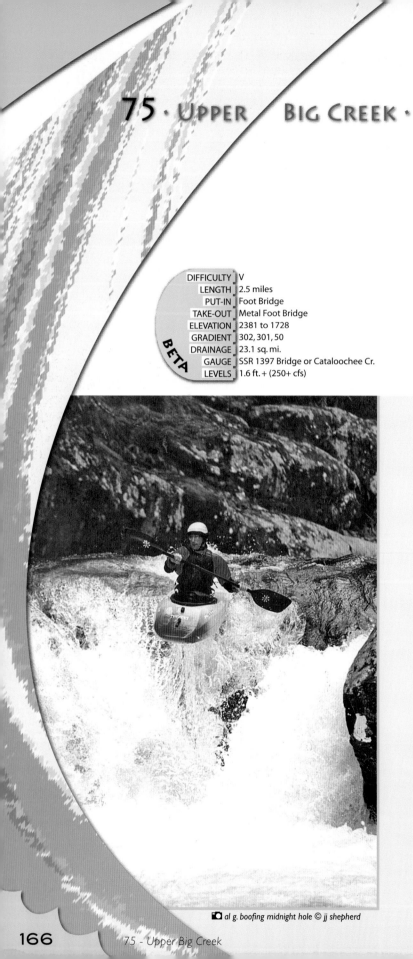
📷 al g. boofing midnight hole © jj shepherd

Upper Big Creek is a super classic Smokies run—made all the more popular by the great scenery, excellent whitewater, one car shuttle, and proximity to both Asheville and Knoxville via the interstate. This is the perfect way to get an afternoon class V fix in the park when you don't have time for a bigger ordeal.

From the parking lot at the top end of the road, walk up the river left trail 2.5 miles to the put in at the concrete bridge, being sure to respectfully stop and step off the trail without startling horses when you meet them—friction between horse packers and kayakers has been building, and we don't want to lose access to this important run. Although plenty of people have gone higher than the concrete bridge, it's the most common spot to start. Putting into the crystal clear creek, paddlers will be greeted by continuous class IV/V that will really not let up for most of the run.

There are three spots where the pace picks up considerably—and boaters should take special note. The first is Monster—a very nasty drop with horrible pin potential on the right side and an undercut to dodge on the left. This rapid can be scouted pretty easily from the trail—it's just upstream of Midnight Hole, just downstream of where the creek rejoins the trail. I was nearly bitten off here a few years ago in a pin on the right side—fortunately the paddler behind me landed on my boat and knocked me free. The

second spot of note is shortly downstream of here—Midnight Hole is a 10 foot vertical drop which has a pretty wicked hole under some overhanging rocks—make sure you boof out pretty far on this one. It is clearly visible from the trail on the walk up. The final thing to be aware of is Action Alley. Not far downstream of Midnight Hole in a section where the creek leaves the trail for a while, the creek drops through 4 major rapids that are bigger than anything else on the creek. They are often littered with wood (like the rest of the run), and should be scouted carefully if you don't have a guide—especially at higher water when they begin to blend together.

The 3/4 mile or so below Action Alley is still continuous fun, but of a slightly easier sort. Lots of folks walk up and run from below Action Alley into the Lower when the water is high.

Shuttle: To reach Big Creek, take exit 451 from I-40 in Tennessee. Cross the river, and turn left heading upstream along the Pigeon. When you reach Big Creek, follow the creek upstream going straight through the stop sign and continuing to the parking lot for the trailhead at the top end of the road. Walk back to the gated road-bed which cut off to the right just before the entrance to the parking area, and hike the roadbed as high as you want to put in.

philip curry at the put in rapid - © boatingbeta.com

76 · LOWER BIG CREEK ·

BETA	
DIFFICULTY	IV
LENGTH	1.9 miles
PUT-IN	Metal Foot Bridge
TAKE-OUT	SSR 1332 Bridge
ELEVATION	1728 to 1444
GRADIENT	180, 104
DRAINAGE	29.4 sq. mi.
GAUGE	SSR 1332 Bridge or Cataloochee Cr.
LEVELS	400+ cfs

Lower Big Creek sports a short section of excellent continuous class IV. It is easily accessible from the interstate, about an hour from Asheville or Knoxville, and runs quite often with a bit of rain in the park. There are no major rapids of note—just one long class III/IV that starts at the put in and finishes at the take out. Beware of the dam dropping into the Pigeon—although it has been run at lower water, it forms a really nasty hole at higher levels. Most folks choose to take out after the left bend above the second bridge you pass under. If you are seeing the power plant—it's definitely time to find an eddy. It's not uncommon for folks to run this gem several times in an afternoon to get a good workout.

Shuttle: To reach Big Creek, take exit 451 from I-40 in Tennessee. Cross the river, and turn left heading upstream along the Pigeon. When you reach Big Creek, follow the creek upstream a short distance and park on the left after crossing the second of two bridges. To reach the git-in, continue upstream, going straight through the stop sign and continuing to the parking lot for the trailhead at the top end of the road.

77 · PIGEON ·

BETA

DIFFICULTY	III
LENGTH	4.4 miles
PUT-IN	Waterville Power Plant
TAKE-OUT	Hartford
ELEVATION	1362 to 1242
GRADIENT	27 fpm
DRAINAGE	Summer and Power Generation
GAUGE	800-899-4435, USGS Pigeon at Waterville
LEVELS	1200cfs +

The Pigeon is a river of paradox. It flows from some of the most pristine wilderness in the East—high in the Balsam Mountains, and it is surrounded by the Great Smoky Mountains National Park. Unfortunately, in between the Balsams and the Smokies the river flows through the town of Canton and the Blue Ridge Paper Products pulp and paper mill, where it is contaminated with the waste of paper making. It then flows into the dioxin laden Waterville Lake before it passes through the flumes to the Waterville Power Plant where it boils forth into the fun filled class III section known as the Pigeon River Gorge. What's more, I-40 passes right along this stretch of river.

lost guide - ©2004 whetstone photography

So why bother with the Pigeon River? Primarily because the play and the character of the river are awesome. It is a lively class III play river with many good play spots—it is a wavewheel heaven. A step down from the Ocoee, it's a good place to learn to play and boat in pushy class III with big waves. There is one class III+ or IV, depending on who you ask and the water level, called Lost Guide. It's on the middle of the run and has a hole in the middle which can be skirted or punched depending on your personality. Another bonus is that the crowds are much thinner than the Ocoee and the guides are much more laid back. Furthermore, because of its proximity to I-40 it is very convenient, and shuttling is easy and quick.

dave simpson throwin' on the pigeon - kevin colburn photo

The run ends in Hartford, Tennessee (beyond is a great beginner class I, II section), a gem of a town with friendly raft guides and boaters and a very chill atmosphere. Spend a day on the Pigeon and you will notice that you have forgotten about I-40 and the pollution and you will know that the spirit of the Pigeon River is still strong.

Andria Baldovin

Shuttle: To reach the take out, take exit 447 (Hartford) and cross to the south (Exxon) side of the interstate. Go left at the T junction, and drive until you find a nice spot along the river (away from private property) to park. To reach the put in, get back on I-40 heading east and take exit 451. Cross the river and make a left, driving up the river to the parking area across Big Creek from Waterville Power Plant.

melinda hendershott - © pisgahwhitewater.com

78 · RAVEN FORK ·

This is the ultimate southeastern hair run. The Raven Fork is a crystal clear stream flowing from the center of the Great Smokies National Park through an incredibly steep mossy gorge of hardwoods and out into the Cherokee Reservation. Due to a drainage that is quite large for a creek this steep, the Raven Fork typically runs 1-3 days after a rain, when the West Prong and other runs in the park have run out. The creek has a classic big drop feel, and essentially boasts a mile of rapids that are as big or bigger than Gorilla on the Green. On my first trip I remember thinking that the put in rapid was the biggest rapid I had ever run. I thought that about a half dozen more drops on this run before the day was over—and my mind was blown by the unbelievable rapids in the lower gorge.

The Raven Fork starts strong and stays strong, with a huge class V known as Anaconda right at the put in. Below that are the fabled drops of Headless Horseman, Mortal Kombat, Elbow Basher, Hale Mary (portage), Wet Willy, and more, before you reach the towering Giant of Big Boy Falls. This drop falls 35 feet, landing between a rock and a hard place. The disgustingly slick and difficult portage is on the right—and will look amazingly appealing to you as you scout the drop.

Below Big Boy all hell breaks loose, with a huge sequence of punching sticky holes to a boof to a slide ending with a rock. The name of this drop has changed several times, with my favorites being "Spinal Adjuster" and "The Chiropractor." Those feeling their years will want to keep portaging on the right after Big Boy. Next up is Mike Tyson's Punch Out—a monster of a drop that will set your hair on fire while simultaneously soiling your shorts. Beware of the eight foot drop in the "entrance"—there is only one small spot where it lands in water—the rest crashes onto rocks.

If you've survived this far, the biggest ones are over—but don't let up your guard. Harjes' rapid is next—a flippy 14 footer that wants to land you on a high brace and remove your arm. The main line is runable with care, or a "sneak" is available around a boulder on the left. The final large rapid of the inner gorge is next—a triple drop called Caveman with some places in the landing that you don't want to be—scout left—realizing that the cave is underneath you at the bottom.

📷 *john grace at the third rapid - tommy hilleke photo*

Below Caveman the river lets up to normal class V (which will feel like flatwater at this point) with one exception—a wood stuffed class V+ undercut/sieve fest called The Mangler—which all but the gnarliest gorge travelers portage on the right. Carefully pick your way through the smaller rapids and wood to the take out—and hope there's cold beer and ibuprofen waiting for you there.

Shuttle: This run is near Cherokee, North Carolina. Due to the tenuous nature of access on tribal lands and the fact that the put in and take out both involve using people's driveways, I have decided not to include directions in this book. If you do know the way, please make sure you bring the appropriate gift for the gentleman who lets us use his driveway at the takeout. Also, be careful of the exposed pipe in the dirt road just after you turn off of the driveway on the way to the put in. Breaking this again will cost us access to this run. Do not leave cars in the put in road if you get stuck— there are people who live up the road who will not be able to get home. If you don't know the way, it is imperative that you hook up with someone who does so that we do not jeopardize access to this gem of a creek.

📷 nate elliot log duckin' - tommy hilleke photo
📷 trip kinney enters caveman - teresa gryder photo

DIFFICULTY	V+
LENGTH	1.5 miles
PUT-IN	End of Trail
TAKE-OUT	First Bridge
ELEVATION	3237 to 2595
GRADIENT	569, 73
DRAINAGE	19.5 sq. mi.
GAUGE	big cove road bridge
LEVELS	10" or above on big cove road bridge

BETA

📷 *trip kinney walks the wood at headless horseman - teresa gryder photo*

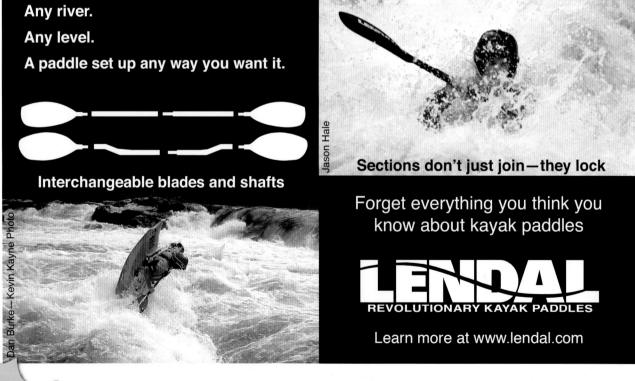

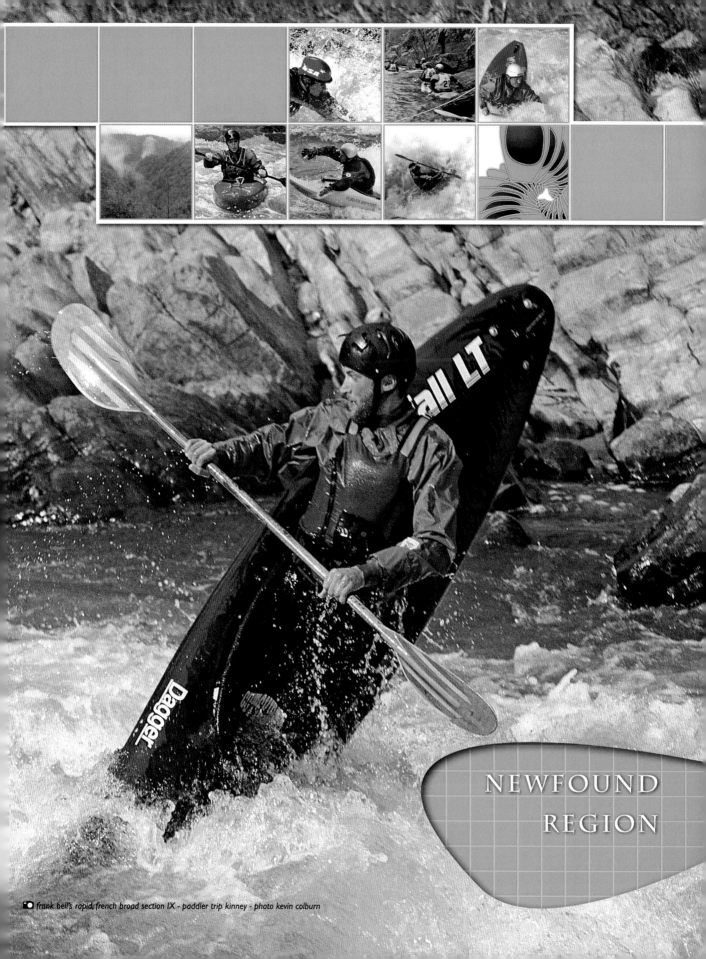

NEWFOUND
REGION

frank bell's rapid, french broad section IX - paddler trip kinney - photo kevin colburn

Nolichucky River

Big Rock

GREENVILLE

107

ERWIN

70/107

Cowbell

Jaws

POPLAR

Davy Crockett
Lake

Nolichucky Gorge

197

Toe
River

Secret
Spot

19w

Huntdale Rd.

107

US 19w

70/208

Cane River

Big Laurel

I-26

BURNSVILLE

25

HOT
SPRINGS

25/70

Section IX

WALNUT

US 19

209

Spring
Creek

Brush Creek

BARNARD

MARS
HILL

French Broad River

213

WEAVERVILLE

MARSHALL

US 25/70

• NEWFOUND REGION •

📷 town falls, spring creek - paddler john pilson - ©LD

79 · BRUSH CREEK ·

DIFFICULTY	IV+
LENGTH	1 mile
PUT-IN	1151 bridge
TAKE-OUT	French Broad
ELEVATION	1754 to 1486
GRADIENT	268
DRAINAGE	7.9 sq. mi.
GAUGE	visual
LEVELS	1000+ on Ivy River Near Marshall (USGS)

ryan bednar photo

Brush Creek, a tributary of the French Broad, is a kind little class IV creek located only about a half hour north of Asheville in Madison County. It takes a steady rainfall to get it running, but due to its constricted nature it can get big in a hurry. Brush Creek is generally running when the Ivy River near Marshall, NC is running 1000 cfs.

It is undeniably tight, moderately steep, and often choked with strainers—as the name implies. Despite the fact that you might find limbs bridging the entire creek near the put-in, it is quite straight forward and fairly kind to errant lines. Unfortunately, it's over just when you get your groove on—the whole run travels only about a mile prior to emptying into the French Broad.

The size of the drops and the easy five minute shuttle invite multiple runs. Alternately, it can be combined with Big Laurel Creek and Spring Creek to form the Madison County Hat Trick, since when one is up the other two will likely be also.

The put-in is on Lower Brush Creek Road where it intersects Barnard Rd near the "town" of Barnard. Parking at the put-in is along the side of the road and on private property. Where possible, every attempt should be made to organize shuttle and leave unnecessary vehicles at the take-out (which also serves as the put in to Section 9 of the French Broad). The creek at the put-in looks impossibly small—little more than a ditch—but small feeder tribs bump up the volume quickly.

There are 4 drops worth mention:

• The 1st drop is a ten to twelve foot drop with two lines. The right line is a technical slide requiring some last minute adjusting, while the left line allows a sweet boof.

• The second drop is a straight forward slide of about 40 feet. Nothing technical here—fast and hard down the middle.

• The third drop looks a bit manky but seems good to go. It consists of a 10 foot slide angling left into a curling pillow which often has lumber in it. Bounce off the pillow and down another 10 vertical feet.

• The last drop is the honey pot that keeps you coming back. It is a slide leading into a vertical drop of about 20 feet. Left of center has a well defined launch pad—just don't land too flat.

When you arrive at the railroad trestle, just walk up the tracks along the French Broad back to the raft put-in at Barnard.

Bob Pfister

Shuttle: From the northern junction of the 25/70 bypass and 25/70 business routes in Marshall, drive north around 3 miles to a left turn on Brush Creek Road, just after the NOC rafting outpost. Follow Brush creek road down and make a left at the T to the put in at the bridge. Continue down this road to the parking area just before the bridge over the French Broad in Barnard. You can hike back up the tracks to here from the confluence of Brush Creek and the French Broad.

80 · SECTION IX ·

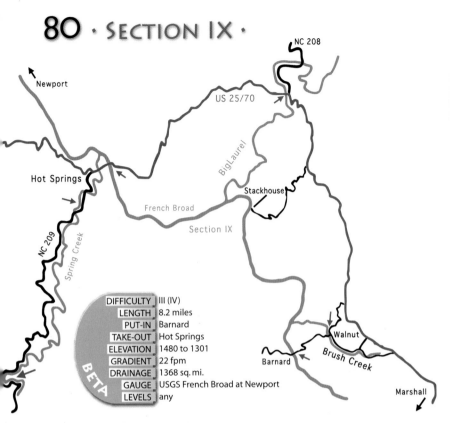

DIFFICULTY	III (IV)
LENGTH	8.2 miles
PUT-IN	Barnard
TAKE-OUT	Hot Springs
ELEVATION	1480 to 1301
GRADIENT	22 fpm
DRAINAGE	1368 sq. mi.
GAUGE	USGS French Broad at Newport
LEVELS	any

Typical southeastern boater's home—confirming the popular myth that they all live in mobile homes and poach for a living.

Section IX is a classic class III run offering up fun rock dodging or stomping big water depending on the recent rains and the time of year. Always runable, this river has some excellent scenery despite the railroad through the valley and the somewhat dirty water from being downstream of Brevard, Hendersonville, and Asheville.

Putting in at Barnard, paddlers will find many fun class II and III rapids on the first half of the river, ending at the Stackhouse. This is often used as a short take out for those wanting to miss the Windy Flats and the two larger rapids below. After the Stackhouse, Windy Flats offers paddlers a great 2 mile flatwater workout—made especially

paddler jeff boggs - © pisgahwhitewater.com

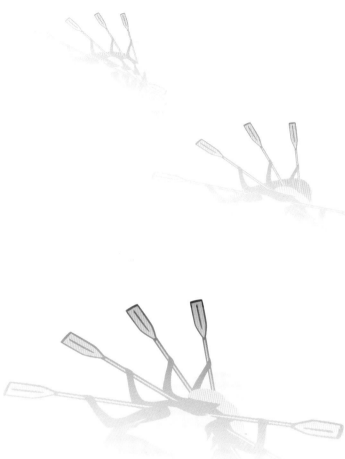

vigorous if there's a headwind. At the end of Windy Flats, the river splits around a very large island. To the right of the island is a class III vertical ledge known as Kayak Ledge or Needle Falls (you will see the tall rock needle on river left from above the island). Kayak Ledge gets a really nasty hole above 10,000 cfs, and increases in difficulty as it gets higher from there. The highest run I've seen was at 67,500 cfs—and it certainly looked class V from my vantage point on the bank. To the left of the island, there is a surfable wave train that also gets progressively better as the water rises.

About 1/2 mile below the island is the biggest rapid on the run—Frank Bell's Rapid. This rapid is nasty at lower levels, but is washed out and completely gone above 20,000 cfs. A sneak is available to the left of some islands for those not ready to kick the difficulty up a notch. Paddle down from here under the tall train bridge to the take out. When the highway bridge comes in sight, be aware that the final rapid—Surprise Ledge—is lurking invisibly across the right 2/3 of the river bed. This drop is fun at lower levels, but can become a terminal hole at higher levels.

Shuttle: Take the 25/70 exit from I-26 in Weaverville, and head north on 25/70 to Hot Springs. This will require one left turn over the Big Laurel. Arriving in Hot Springs, make the last right before the bridge over the French Broad, and circle back under the bridge to the parking lot between the road and the river. To reach the put in, drive back south on 25/70, making a right turn at the T across the Big Laurel. From the T, continue 5.25 miles to a right turn on SR 1151. Follow this road as it winds through several turns in the town of Walnut and descends to the river at Barnard. Park in the lot on the left just before the bridge over the river. An alternate take out is available at the Stackhouse, reached by turning down Stackhouse Road, found 2 miles south of the bridge over the Big Laurel. Proceed to the parking lot on the bank of the river.

📷 *frank bell's rapid, paddler trip kinney - photo kevin colburn*

81 · BIG LAUREL ·

DIFFICULTY	III/IV
LENGTH	3.6 Miles (7 Miles total)
PUT-IN	US 25/70 Bridge
TAKE-OUT	Hot Springs
ELEVATION	1586 to 1358
GRADIENT	63 fpm
DRAINAGE	128.7 sq. mi.
GAUGE	French Broad at Newport - Marshall/US 25 Bridge
LEVELS	2000 cfs / -6 inches to 5 ft on bridge

BETA

Big Laurel is a beautiful class III run that offers a great introduction to creeking at lower levels and a super fun river run at higher levels. There are 3 major drops with tons of other good fun in between. The first major rapid on the run—Stairstep—occurs about a mile into the run. It is best scouted from the trail on the left, which parallels the river from the put in to just below the third big rapid. After Stairstep, it's not too far to the next large one—Suddy Hole. Suddy Hole is the most dangerous rapid on the river, due to a large boxed-in hole on river right. There is a very clean line right down the middle of the slide avoiding the hole. Next up will be the Narrows—two juicy rapids where the water necks down between vertical walls.

Below here, there are quite a few more good rapids down to the confluence with the French Broad—where you will have two options. If you ran shuttle to Hot Springs, paddle the two mile Windy Flats and challenge the bigger water drops of Kayak Ledge and Frank Bell's Rapid. If you want to skip the French Broad, take out at the confluence and carry 1/2 mile up the train tracks to the parking area at the Stackhouse.

Shuttle: To reach the git-in, take US 25/70 north from Weaverville 21 miles to a left turn at the bridge over the Big Laurel. Park just before the turn on the left. For the git-out, continue on 25/70 to Hot Springs. Just before the bridge over the French Broad, take a right and loop back under the bridge. Park in the lot on the right across from the rafting companies. You can also skip the paddle out on the French Broad by hiking the train tracks back upstream from the Big Laurel confluence to the Stackhouse.

📷 *suddy hole - paddler john pilson - ©LD*

📷 *the narrows - paddler john pilson - ©LD*

DIFFICULTY	III/IV- (IV+)
LENGTH	5.1 miles
PUT-IN	FR.
TAKE-OUT	Hot Springs
ELEVATION	1805 to 1399
GRADIENT	86, 82, 100, 82, 51, 5
DRAINAGE	60.9 sq. mi.
GAUGE	French Broad at Newport - Marshall / Hot Springs Bridge
LEVELS	2000 cfs / 0' - 3'

BETA

all photos paddler john pilson - ©LD

Spring Creek is a super scenic class III/IV-run that allows intermediate boaters to have a great wilderness creeking experience without the added pressure of facing large drops. Leaving the bridge at the put in, it flows several miles through a deep wooded gorge with occasional cliff walls rising from the creek before rejoining the highway for a short distance to the take out at Town Falls.

The action on Spring Creek starts right away with some of the most difficult rapids on the run in a gorge about 50 yards down from the put in. After the initial flurry of activity, the river eases up for a bit over the next mile until you reach a river wide shelf where a rock wall rises from the river left side. Scout or carry right. Below here the river hits a pace of class III paddling for miles and miles, with innumerable small ledges that will keep you well entertained. Many of these ledges develop sticky holes at levels above 1 foot—so use caution at high water.

You will notice the difficulty easing as you enter a section with some houses and fields along the creek. This will last until the creek crosses back under the highway and picks up pace for the final rally down to the take out at Town Falls. Town Falls is a large class IV+ drop which you should scout carefully when you run shuttle so that you'll know where to stop. Although the drop has been run many times, most paddlers choose to take out above it. If you want a little more fun, you can paddle down another mile to the bridge in downtown Hot Springs and take out right next to the bar.

Shuttle: From the Spring Creek Bridge in Hot Springs, drive south on NC 209 about a mile to the large obvious class IV+ on the right. Park here for the takeout. To reach the put in, drive another 5.5 miles on 209 to a left turn on FR 233 (Puncheon Camp Rd.) in a sharp curve to the left. Drive this road down to the creek.

83 · NOLICHUCKY ·

DIFFICULTY	III+
LENGTH	8.9 miles
PUT-IN	Poplar
TAKE-OUT	Chestoa Rec Area
ELEVATION	1979 to 1663
GRADIENT	36 fpm
DRAINAGE	607.8 sq. mi.
GAUGE	USGS
LEVELS	500 cfs and up

BETA

The Nolichucky is one of the finest wilderness river runs in the South, with a deep gorge that is only slightly marred by the presence of the railroad. The river's first few miles are littered with class III rapids and play spots—the perfect learning ground for the intermediate river runner and beginning playboater. Although the last few miles ease up a bit in difficulty—there is an abundance of waves here that are perfect for learning to surf—and if you miss one there will likely be another shortly downstream. The Noli is a long day, so bring a lunch, plenty of water, and spare clothes if it's not summer—it can get bitter cold in the afternoons when the sun passes behind the towering gorge walls.

From the parking lot, float downstream under the railroad trestle, stopping to surf the small wave just behind it on the left. In the first bend to the left the rapids start with a fairly straight forward class III. Below that there is a pool, then the well known rapid "On the Rocks." Below On the Rocks is a series of waves down the right bank, then a large stompy hole known as Jaws—the best play spot on the run. After jaws there are a few more smaller rapids before the biggest and most dangerous rapid on the run—Quarter Mile. Quarter mile can be scouted from the left, with a good eddy above the rapid and access to the train tracks if you want to scout its entire massive length. There are two named holes in this rapid—Hungry Jack near the top on the left, and its much worse companion—Murphy's Ledge—a nasty keeper pourover that spans the entire middle of the river at the very bottom of the rapid. This one should be skirted in the rocky stuff on far left or along the base of the small cliff on river right, as it has been the site of several drownings.

Once past Quarter Mile there are many more excellent rapids and surf waves as you travel down this fantastic gorge. The first take out is on river right, where paddlers can pay the campground for over-priced river access, showers, shuttle, and camping. If you want to avoid the hassle at the campground, there is another take out a mile downstream at the Chestoa Rec. Area on the right— where parking is only $2/car.

Shuttle: To reach the take out, take exit 12 from I-26 in Tennessee. Head to the south/east side of the interstate, and take a left at the T. Follow this road past a gas station on the left and through a road cut, slowing down and looking carefully for a right on Chestoa Road. Follow Chestoa road until you cross the river, then take an immediate right and proceed to the take out at Chestoa Rec Area. To reach the put in, return to Chestoa Road and go right, crossing the train tracks and heading into Erwin. After a little over 2 miles, you will merge into 19/23 in Erwin. Follow this until 19/23 makes a left, and go right instead. Go to the first major intersection, and go left, proceeding until this road ends as well. Make a right at the end of this road, and follow it to a left turn with a garage in front of you. At the next T junction, make a right. Follow this road out of town and over the mountain, dropping to the river on the far side. When you see the railroad tracks, make a right onto the dirt road to the river access point.

on the rocks - paddler andria baldovin - ©LD

Jaws is an excellent park and play spot with a short walk that allows for a beautiful setting to enjoy while you wait in line—on the rare occasion that a line forms. This juicy but shallow hole will offer 360s, blasts, and backblasts, as well as serving up some blunts, ends, and loops to skilled paddlers in short boats. The hole consists of a churny pocket on surfer's left that can dish out some beatings if you don't stay in control, and a sweet spot and shoulder on surfer's right where the best rides are usually had. There is eddy service from both sides, and a large recovery pool downstream. Although this hole is an excellent first big hole experience at lower levels, it can get sticky and challenging above 2000 cfs—and at many higher levels you must be upright and in control to exit the feature. At very high levels (above 5000 cfs), this hole forms a much taller, tighter pile and is more of a wave, offering up a variety of bigger water play moves to expert paddlers.

To reach the hole, put in at Poplar and run down about 3/4 mile through the first rapid at a left bend just past the trestle, and the second rapid—"On the Rocks." After On the Rocks there are a couple surf waves down the right bank before the obvious hole at Jaws extends from a river right rock outcrop. Carry back up the train tracks when finished, being careful not to get caught by a train while on the trestle.

Shuttle: From Asheville, drive north on I-26 about 18 miles to the US 19 / Burnsville exit. Take US 19 about 11 miles to a left on US 19 W. Make another left about 1/4 mile up to stay on 19 W, and follow the Cane River just under 15 miles, crossing the river 3 times. Just before the fourth bridge over the river, make a right to continue downstream. Continue downriver 3.75 miles as the road turns at the confluence and heads up the Toe River. Make a left and cross the Toe on the crumbling one lane bridge, continuing through Huntdale a little over a mile to a left across the train tracks on 197. Follow 197 over the mountain and down to the river and train tracks, bearing left on the gravel road where the road again leaves the tracks.

Levels and Gauges: The USGS and TVA both have gauges downstream of the gorge in Embreeville, which give a good indication of what was going on at Jaws 8-12 hours earlier. Levels of 1400 – 2000 are the easiest, and the hole gets really stompy but is still fun from 2000 – 3000. Above this the hole becomes nasty until it forms more of a wave-hole at 5000 – 8000.

leland and gabe hyatt - andria baldovin photo

leland - andria baldovin photo

85 · COWBELL ·

During the writing of this book, two floods of 70,000 cfs inside of two weeks ripped through the Nolichucky Gorge—rearranging many of the rocks and channels at the exit of the gorge, and destroying possibly the finest squirt spot anywhere. Cowbell was the classic Mystery Move spot—a deep seam with a double drop allowing for a huge variety of entrances and rides—giving up some of the longest sub aquatic voyages ever had in a kayak at almost any level. Skilled roamers often sent rides of 20 seconds or more, and almost everyone who tried this spot came up gasping and wide eyed at least once. This was the site of the first mystery move competition—the Angst Mystery Nationals—which brought together over 50 of the world's finest downtime hounds once a year for 6 years to share in the under water fun. Efforts will be made to repair this spot, but due to extensive rearrangement of the river bed it is a strong possibility that Cowbell and all the fun it gave up are gone for good—just a few deep river bottom rocks covered in gel coat where one of the finest play spots ever once was.

Rest in Peace, old friend.

the tall one drops in - ©LD

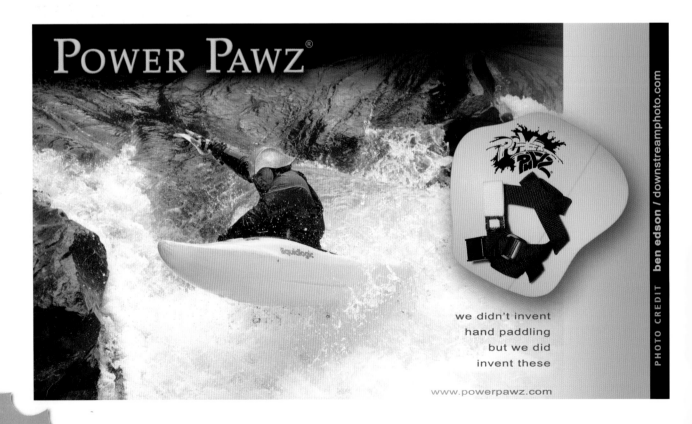

86 · BIG ROCK ·

chris manderson - © pisgahwhitewater.com

Big Rock is a great cartwheel hole that comes out at low water—when most of the other play in the area has run dry. It offers good eddy service and ends and splits—a great way to cool off on a summer day, or to keep your game on between Gauley trips in the fall. In drought years, this spot can be a favorite all year.

Shuttle: Take exit 18 from I-26 in Erwin, TN, and drive north on 81 to a bridge over the Nolichucky. There have been serious access issues in the past—occasionally boaters can access the spot from pullouts downstream on river right, and for a while access was allowed by a private land owner on river left. Check the current situation before trying either of these options. Failing that, you can paddle down .45 miles from the bridge to the hole on river left, and paddle another 2 miles out to the next bridge, which can be reached by car by continuing north on 81.

📷 *chris manderson - © pisgahwhitewater.com*

Gauges and Levels: This spot is less than a mile downstream from the gauge. You can check the USGS online gauge at Embreeville, or the TVA phone gauge by calling 1-800-238-2264 and selecting option 3. The spot is there between 500 and 700 cfs—although it's rocky at the low end and flushy at the high end of that range.

87 · SECRET SPOT ·

"Nona's Secret Spot" wasn't discovered by many until the late 90's because it is so far removed from the other whitewater on the Nolichucky River, and not easily visible from the road. Luckily, the secret is out, as it is the finest frequently running play spot in the Asheville / Knoxville area. Surfable from 1200 to 3500 cfs on the Nolichucky gauge far upstream, the Secret Spot frequently comes in just as your favorite creeks have gone out. If you remember the gage is 12 hours upstream and that 'the sun don't shine on the Secret' you will not be disappointed. Alternately, you can check the new TVA gauge below Nolichucky Dam for levels right at the spot.

Bring a Rope:

String a throw-rope on river left so you can pull / attain back up and enjoy the show as your buds flail in the process.

Clay Wright

Directions:

From the 25/70 split at the Big Laurel put in, head north into Tennessee on 70. About 8.25 miles into Tennessee, look for a left down to the river. If you cross the river, you've gone a bit too far.

The Hole:

A nice wide foam-pile with a sweetly sloping surfer's left shoulder for straight surfing, spinning, and blunting. The center has a shallow spot but cartwheels and loops abound with some practice. Roll up carefully, as there are several rocks just below the surface downstream that break paddles and helmets at lower flows.

photos © pisgahwhitewater.com

NORTHERN
MOUNTAINS

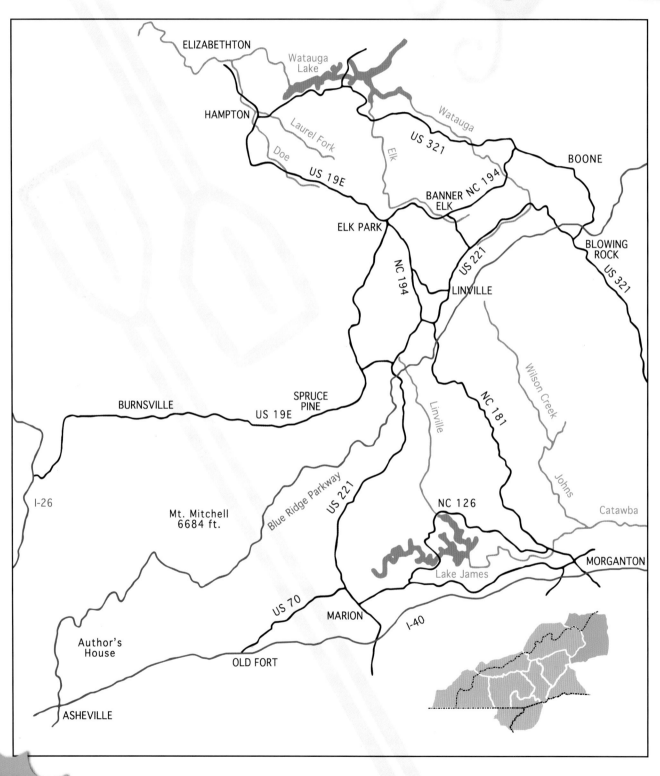

ELIZABETHTON

Watauga Lake

HAMPTON

Laurel Fork

Doe

Watauga

US 321

BOONE

US 19E

Elk

BANNER ELK

NC 194

ELK PARK

NC 194

US 221

BLOWING ROCK

US 321

LINVILLE

Wilson Creek

BURNSVILLE

SPRUCE PINE

US 19E

Linville

NC 181

Johns

I-26

Mt. Mitchell 6684 ft.

Blue Ridge Parkway

US 221

NC 126

Catawba

MORGANTON

Lake James

US 70

MARION

I-40

Author's House

OLD FORT

ASHEVILLE

The good life under Table Rock

187

88 · RED ROOF ·

BETA

DIFFICULTY	IV
LENGTH	1.9 miles
PUT-IN	Shull's Mills
TAKE-OUT	NC 105
ELEVATION	2913 to 2754
GRADIENT	46, 113
DRAINAGE	22 sq. mi.
GAUGE	Watauga River at Sugargrove
LEVELS	500 - 2000

📷 paddler pete pickering ©brian sandefur

The Red Roof is a great resource for a quick run after work or class in Boone if the water is up, with a take out less than 6 miles from the campus of Appalachian State University. The whitewater is fun class IV/V without being super gnarly, and the run is short and mostly roadside, making it a great option for folks wanting to try out some creeking a small step up from the Watauga Gorge. Look for levels between 500 and 2000 at Sugar Grove, and plan to do a few runs if you want to get the most out of your day.

Shuttle: From Boone, drive south on 105 about 4.75 miles to the take out at the bridge over the river. To reach the put in, continue south on 105 another 1.25 to 1.5 miles to a left on SR 1557 at Shulls Mill. Follow the road a short distance to the bridge.

📷 paddler justin hackler ©brian sandefur

89 · UPPER WATAUGA ·

This class II/III run is an excellent option for beginner to intermediate paddlers in the Boone area. The river is wide open, leading to very few surprises on the way down. The largest rapid is found just downstream of the put in, and is visible from the highway. This drop has some nasty spots in it, and is carried more often than not. Use caution when approaching the bridge at the take out—it sits low to the water and can form a strainer at high levels.

Shuttle: From Boone, drive west on US 321 about 11 miles to the put in at a bridge over the river. To reach the take out, continue west on 321 for another 3 miles to Guy's Ford Road on the right. Take Guy's Ford to the take out at the river.

· WATAUGA ·
DRAINAGE

90 · WATAUGA ·

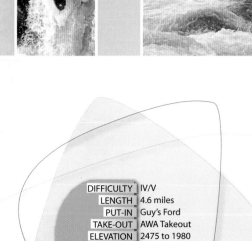

DIFFICULTY	IV/V
LENGTH	4.6 miles
PUT-IN	Guy's Ford
TAKE-OUT	AWA Takeout
ELEVATION	2475 to 1980
GRADIENT	112, 104, 119, 132, 28
DRAINAGE	127.1 sq. mi.
GAUGE	Watauga River at Sugargrove
LEVELS	125+

BETA

The Watauga may well be the best class IV run on Earth, with non stop action for 4 miles in a beautiful wooded canyon setting. The rapids range from technical weaving through complex rapids to blind slots and a million boofs over drops and holes. Boaters familiar with the Upper Yough will feel at home here, and will love the added thrill of the extra gradient. The highlight of the run is Watauga Falls, a 16 foot drop at the state line also known as Stateline Falls or "Tennessee the Hard Way."

Putting in at Guy's Ford Road, there will be about 1/4 mile of warm up before things really kick into gear. About 150 yards past a house high above on a rock outcrop on the left, the river disappears into a maze of boulders which ends in a sneaky hole that is the site of quite a few swims. Below here, there are three more large rapids—the second of which has a nasty but easily avoidable sieve in the center at the bottom. One horizon line later is Hydro—which you will want to scout from the left. It's a long rapid with a boof at the top, several sticky holes in the middle, and a really big hole that must be boofed over at the end.

AMERICAN
AW
WHITEWATER

jeff owen wheels stateline - photo kevin colburn

watauga falls - paddler ken strickland - photo gary dupree, (center inset) philip curry in heavy water ©LD, (right inset) paddler ken strickland - photo chris smith

Below Hydro things ease up a bit, settling into a groove of fantastic rapids that come one after another for miles through this gorge. All of the drops are runable, but there are a large number of places you don't want to be—so scout anything that's blind. You'll know the end is in sight when you reach Watauga Falls; there are only a few rapids left. Be aware that rocks lurk in the left side of the landing at Watauga Falls, so boof right. There will be three more rapids of note—the last of which is a 6 foot drop on the river left side at Rewind—which tradition says should be run backwards your first time down.

Below Rewind, the rapids drop to class III then II, then play out into a pool. Just below the pool the river splits around Watson island, with most of the flow going right— make sure you stay in the small channel on the left. About 200 yards downstream of the split you will notice a flight of wooden stairs up a steep hill about 20 feet back from the river on the left. Take out and carry up the stairs and trail to the AW take out.

Shuttle: To reach the git-in, drive east on US 321 3.1 miles from the state line to Guy's Ford Road. Go left on Guy's Ford to the river. To reach the git-out, drive 2.2 miles west of the state line on 321, and make a right on Tester Road. Follow this road about a mile past some trailers, into a field, around a hairpin left at an old house, and down to the AW takeout.

DIFFICULTY	IV/V
LENGTH	2 miles
PUT-IN	S.R. 1326
TAKE-OUT	Heaton Bridge
ELEVATION	3304 to 3012
GRADIENT	86,206
DRAINAGE	19.3 sq. mi.
GAUGE	Watauga at Sugargrove
LEVELS	700+

BETA

The Upper Elk is a quick roadside run that makes for a great option when the Watauga and Elk are high. The rapids are really fun class IV/V, running through the back yards of several vacation homes. Some drops will require scouts from these yards, meaning it is often best to avoid this run in summer unless you know it well enough that you won't have to scout. Please try your best to stay below the high water mark if you must get out so that we don't lose access to this cool little stretch of creek.

Below the bridge in Heaton, the rapids continue for about 1/2 mile before the river flattens out. You can run down the drops and carry back up to the road if you want to lengthen your run a bit.

Shuttle: From Banner Elk, drive west on 194 2.25 - 2.5 miles to a left on SR 1326. Put in at the bridge over the river. To reach the take out, continue west on 194 to the bridge over the river in Heaton.

paddler shane day - photo brad roberts

compression falls first d - paddler steve frazier

elk river falls - paddler trip kinney - ©boatingbeta.com

leland portaging twisting falls - ©boatingbeta.com

92 · TWISTING FALLS ELK ·

If you have an acute spirit of adventure and you want to go big without going super hard, the Twisting Falls section of the Elk is the run for you. With large bedrock rapids and plenty of vertical waterfalls, the Elk is full of thrills—as long as you don't mind a little bit of a sketchy portage.

From the put in, most folks walk down the trail and put in at the base of Big Falls. This falls was first run in the early '90s by open boater Steve Frazier, whose exploit gave the falls the new title of "Compression Falls." This 55 footer has seen several runs since, resulting in trips to the hospital almost as often as not.

Below Big Falls the river is comparatively tame for quite a ways, before an obvious horizon line marks the beginning of the real fun at a juicy double drop. From here there are several miles of chunky ledges and big slides, which end with a bang at Twisting Falls. This is where the adventure really begins. The final drop before Twisting Falls is an eight foot ledge which angles from upstream river right to downstream river left. It is crucial that you make the eddy on the left below this ledge—the unrunable Twisting Falls is just below. The portage of Twisting Falls is done on a narrow rock ledge high above the constricted 30 foot drop. Scoot along the ledge and use ropes to lower your boats down a gully to the rocks at the base of the falls.

Now for the prize. Peel out and boof left on the next small drop, and eddy out on the left to scout the horizon line below. This 15 footer boasts a meaty hole, and is not too far upstream of Elk River Falls—so set safety and know to swim hard left if you get worked in the hole—the right channel of the falls crashes onto rocks. Elk River Falls is a clean 33 foot drop—a no brainer that requires nothing more than the restraint to not paddle as you go over it. Float off the main flow, lean forward, get your paddle shaft away from your face and get ready for the hard hit—the water is quite green at the base of this one.

paddler danny mongno - ©LD

DIFFICULTY	V
LENGTH	4.8 miles
PUT-IN	Big Falls
TAKE-OUT	Poga Road Bridge
ELEVATION	2766 to 2176
GRADIENT	65, 112, 142, 231, 39
DRAINAGE	44.9 sq. mi.
GAUGE	Watauga at Sugargrove
LEVELS	500+

BETA

The take out bridge is about a half mile and several wide ledges downstream—look out for holes as you make your way to the cooler.

Shuttle: To reach the take out, drive east from Elk Park .5 - .75 miles on 19E to a left turn on 194. Take 194 a little over 3 miles to a left on SR 1124 (Sam Eller Rd.). Follow Sam Eller 2 miles to a stop sign, and go right. Follow this road a little over 6 miles to a left turn on Stoney Hollow Rd. Take Stoney Hollow 4 miles, and pull out on the right before the bridge over the river. To reach the put in, return to Elk Park and head north on SR 1305, following the signs to the Big Falls Trailhead.

93 · LAUREL FORK ·

BETA		
DIFFICULTY	V
LENGTH	4.4 Miles
PUT-IN	Dennis Cove Trailhead
TAKE-OUT	US 321
ELEVATION	2488 to 1862
GRADIENT	44,315,118,122,27
DRAINAGE	20 sq. mi.
GAUGE	Doe at Elizabethton and Dennis Cove Rain Gauge
LEVELS	800 - 1600 / 1.5" + in 12 hours

The Laurel Fork of the Doe is a beautiful stream which parallels the Appalachian Trail through one of the steepest and most rugged gorges in the East. At normal levels, the run is class IV/V, with one monster portage at the end of the gorge. At high water, the difficulty ramps up, making the near impossibility of escape from the gorge a serious factor.

Putting in near the trailhead, you'll float through some easier water on the way down to the foot bridge, with only a few small ledges to break up the riffles. Shortly after the bridge the creek rounds a hard bend to the right and drops off the first major rapid, which can be scouted by scrambling up some rocks on the right. If you have trouble with this rapid, the first exit is at the bottom of the rapid on the left—hike up and over the small ridge to the trail. Below here the rapids increase in frequency, and the gorge begins in earnest. Just after the first section where the walls rise vertically from the river there is a steep trail out on the right. If the water seems high, this is the place to make your escape before entering the virtually inescapable gorge below.

After a 6 foot vertical ledge falling off to the left, eddy left to scout Darwin's Hole—the most serious rapid on the run. This drop cannot be portaged, and safety is very difficult to set. It consists of a tricky entrance leading quickly to a walled-in pour over hole. At normal levels, people have been able to escape the hole both in and out of their boats. At higher water, you should consider a hike out if you're uncertain of hitting your line. Hike up and over the steep ridge on the left, ferry across the river, and climb the steep slope to the trail.

Below Darwin's you are committed to the beautiful inner sanctum of the Laurel Fork, with fantastic rapids and scenery that is second to none. The gorge ends with 60 foot Laurel Falls—which should be portaged right. Stay lower than you think on the portage, as the high trails make for a much longer walk. From the falls down is scenic class II/III, peppered occasionally with strainers that must be skirted or walked. Take out just upstream of the bridge on river left, and walk the highway to the parking lot and your car.

Shuttle: For the git-out, head east through Hampton, TN on US 321 to the trailhead parking area on the right just east of the bridge over the Laurel Fork. To reach the git-in, head back toward Hampton and look for Dennis Cove Road on the left. Take Dennis Cove road over the mountain to the trailhead parking just before a bridge over the Laurel Fork.

dawn powell - ©LD

first rapid - paddler john kiffmeyer - ©LD

darwin hole entrance drop - paddler dawn powell - ©LD

The Doe Gorge is one of the prettiest runs around, despite the fact that it has an old railroad bed running through it, and the fact that many of the high water marks are lined with garbage from the Appalachian communities upstream. The class III and IV rapids of this run play a wonderful accompaniment to the towering cliff walls which rise hundreds of feet above in the middle of this unforgettable gorge.

From the put-in, paddle for a good while through the flats and into the beginnings of the river gorge. When you pass under two abandoned railroad trestles in succession, you'll know the action is about to pick up. The only rapid of consequence on this stretch—Body Snatcher—occurs about half way through the run. It's marked by a horizon line split by a giant rock in the middle of the river. You can climb out and scout from the rock, but it is advisable to have someone walk down the left bank and hold a rope at higher water—the final hole can be a really sticky one.

Below here there is one more rapid of note—Flag Pole—a juicy one along the left bank at a wall supporting the old railroad bed. The river splits around an island at the top of the rapid, with the main flow going left. Scout from the island.

After Flag Pole, the river eases in difficulty even as the scenery improves—giving you time to appreciate the magic of the Doe Gorge. Stay in your boat on the paddle out—the banks are lined with private property on both sides.

Shuttle: To reach the git-in, head south on 19A out of Hampton, TN about 6.5 miles to Blevins. Make a left in Blevins, and wind your way down river toward the Blevins Bridge. For the git-out, head back towards Hampton and pull out just downstream of where the Doe crosses under 19.

📷 *john kiffmeyer - ©LD*

DIFFICULTY	IV
LENGTH	6 miles
PUT-IN	Blevins
TAKE-OUT	Hampton
ELEVATION	2297 to 1791
GRADIENT	40,111,76,141,92,46
DRAINAGE	60.4 sq. mi.
GAUGE	Doe at Elizabethton
LEVELS	400+

BETA

📷 *john kiffmeyer enters body snatcher - ©LD*

95 · LINVILLE GORGE ·

Linville Gorge is the grand patriarch of all east coast wilderness runs, and provides a level of adventure that is unparalleled in this area. On top of that it boasts the finest scenery to be found—traveling over 16 miles in a two thousand foot deep super rugged rock walled gorge—with over 10 of those miles being hair raising class V. It also runs frequently, and is only 45 minutes from Asheville.

Although early runs through the gorge took 2 days, the run has been made more accessible by the use of alternate put ins and take outs, as well as by the fact that there is now a small community of people who have memorized all of the lines. For those who know it well, a time of 6-7 hours is not uncommon from the Falls to the Lake. The river can be shortened more by carrying down the Babel Tower trail to put in at the beginning of the class V, and by carrying out on the Conley Cove Trail about 1/2 mile below Cathedral Falls. No matter how small a section you bite off, it is still highly advisable that you go with a good guide, since every rapid has at least one deadly sieve or spot that you really don't want to be. Make sure you bring a break down and know the exit points—this river eats boats and paddles on a very regular basis, and it's not uncommon for even the best boaters to occasionally exit the gorge early by foot.

To put in at the falls, park at the river right trailhead and walk the trail toward the river, making a left at the fork and continuing to the observation platform above the falls. Follow a small trail to the right of the platform, skirting one gully and dropping down the next to the water. Despite the intimidating put in, the first three miles is easy class II and III—winding through a beautiful section of Gorge known as "The Bends." This section has only three larger rapids to contend with—all of which are class IV. After the last of these drops, it's only about a half mile until the Babel Tower trail hits the river, and the feces begins to hit the proverbial wind machine. The first class V is a super juiced up 12 foot slot with a nasty looking corner pocket on the left.

Below here the river will become a blur to first timers—with more class IV+ and V rapids than any sane person would run in a day. Use caution all the time—most of the rapids have horrible sieves, and several times an innocent looking channel will disappear completely under the rocks—with no last chance eddies. There are three sections where the difficulty will pick up dramatically, and a good guide is the best way to know where you stand. When you reach the 16 foot drop of Cathedral Falls at the end of the very intense Cathedral Gorge, you'll know the worst is over. Don't let down your guard, though—there are about a half dozen more class V's spread out over the next three miles, and you'll probably be feeling less than fresh at this point. The good news is that the rapids spread out enough for you to check out the best scenery in the gorge on this section. Save some strength and snacks for the 3-4 mile flatwater paddle out as well—and make sure you don't have anything important to do the next day.

Shuttle: To reach the git-out, take exit 90 from I-40 and head north on Harmony Grove Rd. Just North of the interstate, make the first right which is signed to Lake James State Park. Continue on about 2.25 miles, bearing left at the fork 1.25 miles into the drive. Go straight through the intersection at US 70, and then right onto 126 at the next intersection in Nebo. Continue just under 10 miles on 126 to a left turn just before the narrow bridge over the river. To reach the git-in, backtrack about 3.25 miles on 126 to the first right turn. Take this road all the way to Linville Falls. **WARNING**: if you don't have decent clearance and possibly 4x4 (depending on the season) you will need to take 126 west to 70, 70 west into Marion, 221 north to Linville falls, and then go right on 183 and follow the signs to Linville Falls.

📷 *robin betz on the cave falls slide - ©LD*

📷 *entering the jailhouse - paddler curtis burge - ©LD*

cave falls - paddler sven johnson - ©LD

BETA	
DIFFICULTY	V
LENGTH	16.5 Miles
PUT-IN	Linville Falls
TAKE-OUT	126 Bridge
ELEVATION	3088 to 1239
GRADIENT	50, 75, 78, 98, 143, 226, 246, 226, 159, **
DRAINAGE	44.4 sq. mi.
GAUGE	Linville near Nebo
LEVELS	2.0 - 2.9 feet
	**185, 94, 95, 67, 33, 37, 25, 12

chris harjes slides out of the cave falls gorge - ©LD

LINVILLE GORGE SCALE

95.2 · LINVILLE LESSONS ·

"Like a child who,
being in a constant condition of wonder,
is surprised by nothing."

George McDonald

WICK'S IDEA was that white water sport could be elevated in likeness to classic alpine exploration, a la Shipman and Messner, engendering sagas of journeys to the world's most fabulous regions. I, however, was enthused simply to push the limits of what could be paddled, and to explore the uses of these most highly maneuverable, shoulder-carried water craft. Wick Walker and I were high school friends, and we appreciated each others' fantasies. Our confidence derived from our having joined the brave few who paddled the Upper Yough a couple of years before. In the early seventies, rapids like Iron Ring on the Gauley were commonly considered dangerous, at the fringe of possibility.

In the late sixties, a popular guidebook called Appalachian White Water, by Walter Burmeister, was in wide circulation. Within the five hundred or so pages an abundance of unknown rivers materialized in great detail for naïve readers. Expansive descriptions included details of rhododendron covered valleys, profoundly carved canyon walls, and serpentine and steeply dropping waters. Our free hours between school studies were spent poring over these descriptions and imagining what the rivers would be like to boat. So willing were we that we hardly noticed the repetitiousness of the descriptions, written no doubt from the purview only of an armchair and a stack of topo maps. The Linville Gorge, with a drop of nearly 300 ft./mi., soon became central in our dreams of extreme and forbidding rivers. It only took the next fall storm to send us with our 13 ft. fiberglass, self-constructed slalom boats on the drive to the Linville.

We woke up to a bright morning—after a late night of driving, and sleeping a few hours in the front seat of Wick's car—looking out over the parking lot near a beautiful, two step falls. Soon we were sliding our boats down the steep bank at the foot of the falls. The river had barely sufficient water to paddle—perhaps 150-200 cfs. At first the going was relatively easy, and we covered some miles. Then rocks along the shore started to rise and close in, and water began to fall away in earnest.

From that point we scouted nearly every rapid, agonizing somewhat over the consequences of slamming our boats into each new pile of rocks. What were the real limits to this kind of paddling, we wondered, where river was more rock than water? Each rapid required precision. We carefully kept a count of rapids carried, which afterwards was to give us some measure of success. Sometimes I ran first, sometimes Wick. The pace was very slow.

Around 2 PM we came to a fairly vertical 15' falls landing in a jumble of barely submerged rocks. We scouted the landing and thought we could identify a weakness in the barrier of rocks at the bottom, where the water seemed to flow through. Wick went first, and with his high C-1 bow slid smoothly through, hardly touching anything. Encouraged by this, I lined up in my high volume slalom kayak and carefully dropped over. "Crunch!" I was slammed to a complete stop. My bow was caught under a rock, and my back deck started to sink under the weight of water flowing over the falls. It was my first experience of a bow pin. I used my paddle to try to push boat and body back upstream to take the pressure off my bow, but no avail. I started to feel pressure against my back, squeezing me further into my kayak and doubling me forward.

I had made this boat myself out of epoxy resin and layers of fiberglass cloth - Kevlar had not yet been invented. I had the idea that the stuff would break. With a surge of desperate energy, I drove my legs and my body up against the deck, breaking through the fiberglass, and was able to get my legs and feet free. Then I quickly swam over to Wick who was waiting with a rope.

That was the end of the day's paddling. As I climbed out of the water, I found the cockpit dangling free around my waist. I also found that in the process of coming through the deck, I was stripped of one shoe and my swim trunks. The boat and paddle we were able to free. The only problem was that we were in a populated National Park, and I still had to walk out up the path, passing hikers and whole families on the trail without being arrested. Fortunately, I still had my skirt and wore it low, like a Scotsman's kilt.

As we drove back home and discussed the trip, we agreed that far more wearying than any physical stress was the emotional stress of constant decision-making and running rapids we weren't sure were runable. We carried 22 times in about 6 miles.

~~~~~~~~~~

The Linville was still on my hit list in '72 when my little brother Jamie came home from the Olympics with a Bronze Medal. Although he was six years my younger, I figured that if he was good enough to get a Bronze Medal he was qualified to run the Linville Gorge with me. He was familiar with the Linville also, having visited the area on an overnight hiking trip with his summer camp years before. His memories still seemed to be impressed by some of the campfire stories told about the Brown Mountain lights and a couple of Marines who went crazy after being trapped along the river for a week by rising water. The Linville had his attention as a potentially spooky place.

It took another good storm to bring us back, this time in early March, 1973. My girlfriend, Peggy, drove with us in a VW van. We put in on a river with a good bit more water than before, maybe 300 - 400 cfs, and we started early, under graying skies and increasing winds. Jamie was in his 13' slalom boat that he had raced in Europe. I had built another boat, and it had already suffered damage and been patched.

Jamie, Wick and I had worked out a kind of ethic which was meant to dampen any competitiveness between us. Each person was to take complete responsibility for his own decisions, and each agreed to respect and support the decision made by any other— even if the decision was to turn around and hike out. As Jamie said, there was no place for 'being brave'; it only mattered to 'be right.' We didn't want anyone to be pressured into a poor decision.

We ran what chutes and falls seemed feasible until well into the afternoon, and pounded into rocks when errors were made. There came a certain point that my boat was filling up too quickly, and I couldn't go on. It was near the Devil's Hole Trail that led out of the gorge on river left. On the right, the main road followed the river 1000' above where we were expecting Peggy to patrol for us. We decided that Jamie would go on downriver until he got to a trail that led up to the road, and hike up to find our shuttle vehicle. He would then drive around to meet me at the campground put-in.

I hiked up and out for miles, came to an inhabited cabin, borrowed a couple of books of matches, and before dark caught a ride back to the put-in. Jamie returned to the routine of scouting and paddling. He may have made a mile or two more before hiking out on river right just short of Wiseman's View. He was brought up to an empty parking lot at the overlook just at dark. That night, temperatures dropped and snow began to fall. Jamie was stranded in the parking lot with no matches or survival gear. He was wearing a full wetsuit, a spray jacket, and neoprene booties. He only had a plastic racing helmet on his head. Trying to make himself a little more comfortable, he dragged some newspaper out of a trash can, laid it on the concrete floor of an outhouse, stuffed his jacket with dry leaves, and lay down to wait for morning. His only distractions were memories of camping in that very place ten years before, and the awe and solitude he had felt with the gorge.

Being blessed with the means to start a fire, I wasted no time making myself comfortable in the empty put-in parking lot. I gathered every sort of tree limb and trunk I could move and set it all ablaze. Then after some time, I divided the burning limbs and the coals into two parts, and lay down between the two fires in a couple of inches of warm mud that the fire had melted. Here I spent the night, surrounded by the heat of the fire and pleasantly enjoying the feel of the snow flakes melting on my skin. From time to time I would have to get up to rearrange and re-stoke the fires, but then I could fall asleep again in comparative bliss.

By Noon the next day, Jamie, Peggy and I managed to reunite. Jamie's face and hands were flushed crimson and swollen from the night's exposure, and I was covered in mud. Peggy had been taken in by a family living in a cabin at the takeout.

The rest of the day we spent resting and gorging ourselves, and then we had a good night's sleep. The next morning with renewed resolve, and armed with new rolls of grey tape, we took off again in separate directions to reclaim our boats and resume our journey. We told Peggy that this time we would surely make it to the end. At about Noon we had found our boats, re-taped them, and joined up on the river. Thence began again the process of agonizing decisions—scouting almost every rapid, trying to judge what was in the realm of the possible, and trying to protect against impacting our fragile conveyances. Several times we would have to stop, wait for boats to dry, and refresh the taping job of the morning.

Still we continued on without arriving. The shadows lengthened down the walls of the gorge and dark closed in around us. We held on as long as possible to the idea that we would make it to where the river slackened up, and race down the last few miles of easier river before dark. We were near to the Conley Cove Trail when we had to give it up. As soon as we got off the water and under the rhododendron it was full night, and it was impossible to see. We could only feel the path with our feet. Several times we lost the trail and were able to find it only by building a fire. This had to be repeated several times. By the time we made it to the road at the top, it was after midnight, and by the time we hiked down the road to the take out where our van and Peggy were waiting it was nearly dawn.

This was the last time we paddled the Linville. We carried about eight times and ran over half the distance. After this, other challenges caught us up, and the opportunity of water level and time never presented itself again. Our adrenaline habit was fed on the Upper Blackwater, Great Falls on the Potomac, and then a trip to Bhutan. For us, the Linville stood as a nominal defeat—we never made it to the end—but it made us understand precision paddling, and it made us dream of boats that wouldn't break.

Tom McEwan

Editor's Note: Although Tom and Jamie did not make it to the end of Linville Gorge, they did complete the meat of the run through Cathedral Gorge to the Conley Cove Trail, which is now commonly used as a take out.

· WILSON CREEK DRAINAGE ·

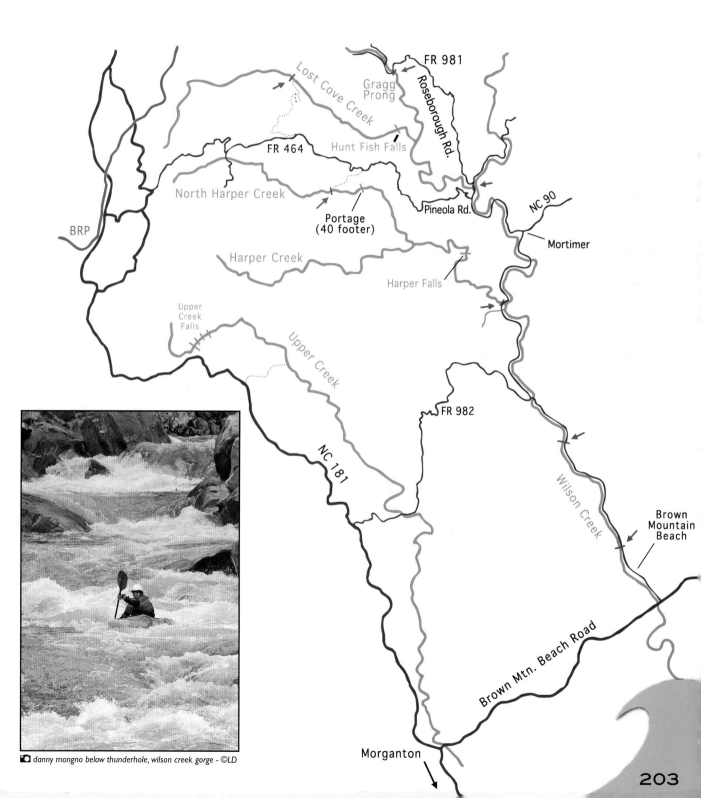

FR 981

Gragg
Prong

Roseborough Rd.

Lost Cove Creek

Hunt Fish Falls

FR 464

North Harper Creek

Pineola Rd.

NC 90

Mortimer

Portage
(40 footer)

Harper Creek

Harper Falls

BRP

Upper
Creek
Falls

Upper Creek

FR 982

NC 181

Wilson Creek

Brown
Mountain
Beach

Brown Mtn. Beach Road

Morganton

danny mongno below thunderhole, wilson creek gorge - ©LD

203

96 · GRAGG PRONG ·

DIFFICULTY	IV+ - V
LENGTH	4.4 miles
PUT-IN	Roseboro
TAKE-OUT	Edgemont
ELEVATION	2131 to 1579
GRADIENT	178,241,52,70,11
DRAINAGE	5.1 sq. mi.
GAUGE	Visual and Adako Bridge Wilson Creek Gauge
LEVELS	Wilson Creek 2'+ or Visual at Roseboro FS981 Bridge

Before paddling the Gragg Prong, I had heard for a couple years of the big easy slides and rapids of this tiny class IV+/V- tributary high in the Wilson Creek drainage. The usual thinking on the Gragg Prong is that if there is enough water to scrape a boat down the creek at the put in, the run will be good to go. Our group arrived to find the creek out of its banks, and waited 3.5 hours for the water to drop to a sane level before putting on. When we finally did put on, the level was about 6 inches below the top of the concrete platform on the upstream river right bridge support—about 1-2 inches above the small concrete lip that runs all the way along the river right support. This felt like a medium high level—you could certainly go higher, but the holes would start to get sticky, and the big drop would be insane.

The Gragg Prong with good water turned out to be a class V wilderness adventure with several portages, lots of wood, and huge powerful drops culminating with The Dragstrip—a towering behemoth of a slide dropping a very steep sixty vertical feet over ledges, through explosions, curlers, and roostertails and into a massive hole. Oceana is for sissies! Whether you choose the right or the left line, be ready for some serious action at this drop—it has broken legs and ribs in the past. The rest of the run consists of several boulder garden style rapids and about a half dozen other large sliding rapids, all but one of which occur before Dragstrip. All of the drops can be scouted or portaged on the Mountains to Sea Trail, which parallels the river on the left. Below the final large rapid, there is a flat but beautiful 2.25 mile paddle out to Edgemont on Lost Cove Creek.

Shuttle: To reach the git-out, follow Wilson Creek upstream from the Brown Mtn. Beach Rd. bridge 8.5 miles to Mortimer. Make a left in Mortimer, and continue 2 more miles to the Bridge over Lost Cove Creek in Edgemont. For the git-in, make a left on Roseborough Rd. (FR 981) just past the bridge over Lost Cove Creek. Drive 4.2 miles and git-in at the bridge over the Gragg Prong just before Roseborough.

📷 andria baldovin speeding on a high water dragstrip - ©LD (left) 📷 chris clark runs safety for jim otto at the cave (left inset) 📷 ping prong - paddler adam mckinney - ©LD (above)

paddler: barry kennon / photo: matt johnson

97 · LOST COVE CREEK ·

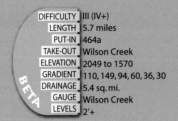

DIFFICULTY	III (IV+)
LENGTH	5.7 miles
PUT-IN	464a
TAKE-OUT	Wilson Creek
ELEVATION	2049 to 1570
GRADIENT	110, 149, 94, 60, 36, 30
DRAINAGE	5.4 sq. mi.
GAUGE	Wilson Creek
LEVELS	2'+

BETA

Lost Cove Creek is a beautiful way for intermediate paddlers to get a true wilderness creeking experience. Set in the wilds of the upper Wilson Creek drainage, this little stream winds through a spectacular wooded valley—falling over several class III rapids and one large class IV along the way. Make sure there has been plenty of rain to get this thing going, and realize that half of the flow you see at the take out is coming from the Gragg Prong, which flows into Lost Cove Creek about 2 miles upstream. The largest rapid on the run—Hunt Fish Falls—is found about half way down, with some decent class III rapids just below. Scout the double drop from river right.

Shuttle: To reach the take out, drive north from Brown Mountain Beach on Wilson Creek 7.7 miles to the junction with 90 in Mortimer. Go left another 2.1 miles to the bridge over Lost Cove Creek in Edgemont. For the put in, backtrack 0.2 miles to Pineola Road. Take Pineola Road 4.9 miles to 464a on the right. Carry 2.3 miles and 862 vertical feet down to the creek.

paddler jimmy ellis ©dennis huntley

BETA		
DIFFICULTY	III/IV (V+)
LENGTH	5.7 miles
PUT-IN	Mtn. To Sea Trail
TAKE-OUT	Wilson Creek
ELEVATION	2238 to 1443
GRADIENT	258, 137, 88, 131, 102, 79
DRAINAGE	4 sq. mi.
GAUGE	Wilson Creek
LEVELS	2'+

Although super scenic, this creek is really only worth paddling if you intend to run the massive Harper Creek Falls in the middle of the run. Hiking down the trail to the small creek, you will put in and paddle a short distance before the first portage at a gnarly necked down 40 footer. Carry on the trail on river right. Below here, the creek is mostly class III/IV past the confluence with Harper Creek until you reach the horizon line at Harper Creek Falls—be wary of wood along the way. This drop should be scouted or carried on the left. It involves a 12 foot drop, getting in a stroke or two, then plunging another 30 near vertical feet. If you're in the wrong place, you're going to get stuffed into a wall on the bottom drop. Below is another 15 foot exit slide. The creek mellows to class III/IV again to the takeout.

Shuttle: To reach the git-out, drive north from Brown Mountain Beach on Wilson Creek 5.8 miles to the one lane bridge over Harper Creek. To reach the git-in, continue north another 1.9 miles to the junction with 90 in Mortimer. Go left another 1.9 miles to Pineola Road. Take Pineola road 3.6 miles to the North Harper Shortcut Trailhead. Hike the Mountains to Sea Trail 0.7 miles and 306 vertical feet down to the river.

99 · WILSON CREEK ·

danny mongno at 10 foot falls (left)
dawn powell runs stairstep (left-center)
kevin colburn in a snowy thunderhole (right-center)
andria cruising downstream (right)

Wilson Creek is a treasure in the class IV world—with fantastic rapids, California style rock slab scenery, easy access, and clean water. The creek has a large watershed and is well channelized, maximizing the days that it runs and the levels at which it can be navigated. Due to this, it is a favorite with intermediate and advanced boaters alike, who flock to the gorge to boof, slide, and punch the many holes found on this excellent creek.

Putting in from the pullout 2.3 miles upstream of Brown Mountain Beach, paddlers will weave through a few small ledges, and skirt a rocky area through some slots on the right. Immediately below here, the pace picks up as the river curves to the left through a steep rapid and drops over 10 Foot Falls. This one is visible from the road on the way up—and is best scouted on the drive due to the long approach and relatively blind entrance. Below here the pace stays good, with lots of excellent class III and several fun class IVs such as Boatbreaker, Triple Drop, and Razorback. Be aware that although Wilson Creek is a moderate run at levels below six inches, the push really picks up and the holes get worse at higher water, giving this creek a class V rating at levels above 1 ft.

Shuttle: To reach the take out, drive north on 181 from the 126 junction in Morganton 10.75 miles to Brown Mountain Beach Road on the right, just before the church. Make a right on Brown Mountain Beach Road, and go 4.8 miles to the bridge over Wilson Creek. Cross the bridge and make a left along the creek. Continue a couple miles until you pass Brown Mountain Beach. Take out at a pullout either 0.2 or 0.6 miles above the Brown Mtn. Beach Entrance. For the put in, drive to the pullout 2.3 miles above Brown Mountain Beach.

DIFFICULTY	IV (-9" - 1') V (1'+)
LENGTH	2.1 miles
PUT-IN	2.3 miles above brown mtn. Beach
TAKE-OUT	first river access above brown mtn. Beach
ELEVATION	1361 to 1119
GRADIENT	80, 117, 45
DRAINAGE	60.9 sq. mi.
GAUGE	BMB Road Bridge
LEVELS	-9 inches to 2'

BETA

ASHEVILLE

downtown asheville with mt. pisgah in the background - ©LD

mefford williams manufactures cartwheels at 88 dodgers - ©LD

Ledges Park is a between—class or after-work quickie paddling destination adjacent to Asheville—if you don't mind the smell. Comprised of a series of ledges spread out over about 200 yards of river, this spot also has the poor fortune to be located 3.5 miles downstream of the Asheville Metropolitan Sewer District's wastewater treatment plant. Nonetheless, it is used daily by Asheville paddlers who come to work out by doing attainments through the rapid, or as a play spot by those bold enough to risk flipping over.

The Shit Hole, found just upstream of the parking area on river right, lives up to its name in both a paddling and olfactory sense. This shallow hole is good for beginners who wish to learn some side surfing and spins. It is best not to try to throw ends in this hole unless you are an expert, and it is also highly advisable that you make sure you are wearing a good helmet before entering the hole—high speed high impact windowshades are a distinct possibility.

The cartwheel spot—88 Dodgers—is the next play feature reached on the way upstream. The feature is located between two rocks—with the pocket being alongside the rock found on the surfer's right. Although a suitable spot for expert lefty end throwers, it should be noted that manufacturing cartwheels here is a task as daunting as that which the Dodgers faced to win the Series back

in '88. Nonetheless, over the years several US Freestyle Team members have made this a stop on their regular training rotation.

Finding the spots: Navigation is easiest using a row of metal posts atop concrete bases which jut up from the river bed along the right side. Counting from the picnic tables, Shit Hole is next to the second post as you head upstream, and 88 Dodgers is about 50 yards upstream of the third post.

When to go: There is something to do at The Ledges any time, but certain levels are better for the play spots than others. For optimal surfing at Shit Hole, look for levels of 2250 cfs and up on the French Broad at Asheville USGS or TVA Gauge. For 88 Dodgers, 1750 - 3500 cfs is the best range. Above 3500 a set of waves at the top of the Ledges begin to form up nicely, reaching their best above 5000 cfs.

Shuttle: From Asheville, head west on I-26 to the Elk Mountain/Woodfin exit. Go left at the top of the ramp, and continue through the small town (watch your speed!) until the road ends at Riverside drive. Go right on Riverside Drive, bear left at the stop sign after 2.2 miles, and continue about another 1-1.5 miles to the Ledges Park parking area on the left.

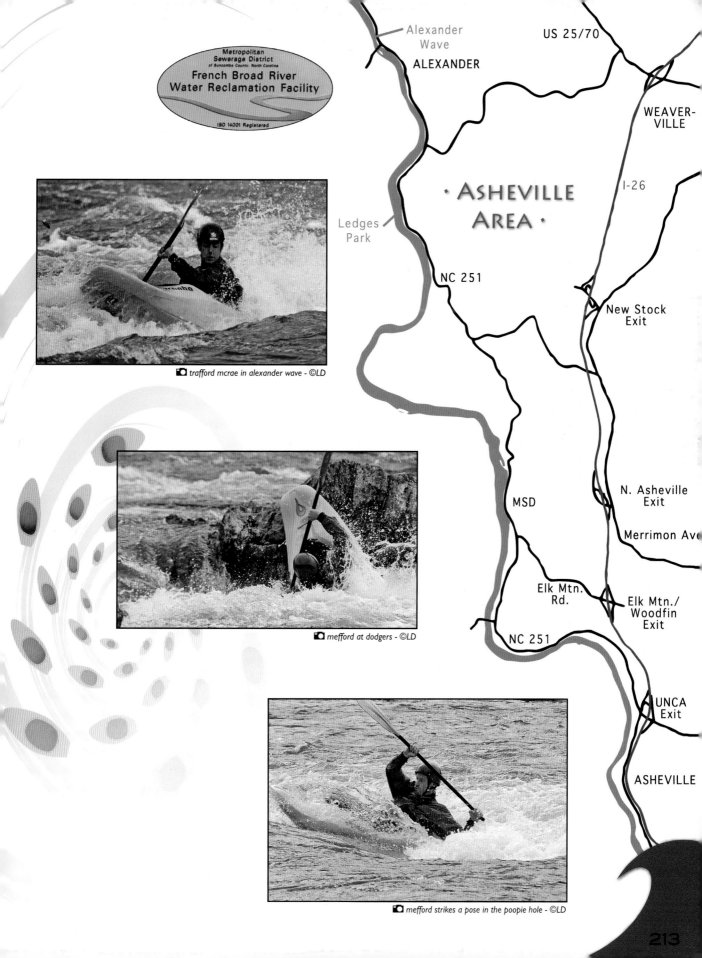

Metropolitan
Sewerage District
of Buncombe County, North Carolina
French Broad River
Water Reclamation Facility

ISO 14001 Registered

Alexander
Wave
ALEXANDER

US 25/70

WEAVER-
VILLE

I-26

· ASHEVILLE
AREA ·

Ledges
Park

NC 251

New Stock
Exit

📷 *trafford mcrae in alexander wave - ©LD*

MSD

N. Asheville
Exit

Merrimon Ave

Elk Mtn.
Rd.

Elk Mtn./
Woodfin
Exit

NC 251

📷 *mefford at dodgers - ©LD*

UNCA
Exit

ASHEVILLE

📷 *mefford strikes a pose in the poopie hole - ©LD*

101 · ALEXANDER WAVE ·

trafford mcrae working alexander wave - ©LD

Alexander Wave is a great park and play option close to Asheville if you don't mind a little smelly water. Located on the French Broad downstream of Asheville at the small town of Alexander, this feature is formed by some slabs of concrete lurking under the river's surface. This tends to form a feature which ranges from a wave to a hole and back, and is best between 3000 and 4000 cfs (French Broad at Asheville). Lower than that you start to hit the concrete, and higher the eddy service starts to get a little more slim.

Make sure you park in the pullout just upstream of the bridge on river right, and be respectful of the private property which borders this spot on all sides.

Gauges and levels: Look for levels between 2000 and 4000 cfs on the French Broad at Asheville USGS or TVA gauges.

Shuttle: From Asheville, head west on I-26 to the Elk Mountain/Woodfin exit. Go left at the top of the ramp, and continue through the small town (watch your speed!) until the road ends at Riverside drive. Go right on Riverside Drive and continue just over 5.5 miles to the town of Alexander, bearing left at the one stop sign. Park just upstream and river right of the bridge in Alexander. DO NOT PARK ON RIVER LEFT! The play spot is downstream of the bridge on river left.

APPENDIX

· RUNS BY DIFFICULTY ·

Following are lists of all runs in the book in order of difficulty from easiest to hardest, first by region and then overall. In order to allow for more differentiation, the difficulty scale has been expanded to 6—with three of the runs in the book rating a 6 or higher. It is worthy of note that runs rated 6.0 are at the highest limits of class V on the International Scale of River Difficulty. The one run rated at 6.25 would fall into the class VI rating on that scale. All measures of difficulty are highly subjective—although I have made my best effort at rating these accurately, use this information as a general guide only.

Reach#	River	Region	Difficulty	Page
7	Lower Green	1	2	44
4	Upper Green	1	3.75	40
5	Big Hungry	1	4.5	41
3	Green River Dries	1	4.75	39
1	Upper Rocky Broad	1	5	36
8	North Pacolet	1	5	47
2	Rocky Broad	1	5.5	37
6	Green Narrows	1	5.5	42
9	Dupont	1	5.75	48
10	Upper Davidson	2	3.5	51
13	Upper NF French Broad	2	4.5	55
14	North Fork French Broad	2	4.5	56
12	Courthouse Creek	2	4.75	55
15	West Fork French Broad	2	4.75	58
11	Looking Glass Creek	2	5	52
17	Upper West Fork Pigeon	2	5.25	62
19	West Fork Pigeon	2	5.25	64
21	Bathtubs	2	5.25	66
16	Big East Fork	2	5.5	60
20	Middle Prong	2	5.5	65
18	Garden of the Gods	2	6.25	63
29	Section II	3	2	87
30	Section III	3	3.5	88
27	Chauga	3	4.5	83
22	Eastatoe	3	4.75	69
31	Section IV	3	4.75	90
32	Tallulah	3	4.75	92
34	Middle Cullasaja	3	4.75	99
28	Overflow	3	5.25	86
26	Upper Whitewater	3	5.5	78
33	Upper Cullasaja	3	5.5	98
23	Toxaway	3	5.75	72
24	Horsepasture	3	5.75	74
25	Silver Run Falls	3	5.75	77
35	Lower Cullasaja	3	5.75	100
38	Tuckasegee	4	2	108
39	Little Tennessee	4	2	109
43	Nantahala	4	3	114
42	Upper Nantahala	4	3.5	113
36	West Fork Tuck	4	4	106
41	Cascades	4	4.75	111
40	Whiteoak Creek	4	5.5	110
57	Hiwassee	5	1.75	138
49	Lower Santeetlah	5	3.5	126
55	Middle Tellico	5	3.75	134

Reach#	River	Region	Difficulty	Page
58	Upper Ocoee	5	3.75	139
61	Ocoee	5	3.75	142
46	Lower Snowbird	5	4	123
53	Citico Creek	5	4	131
56	Coker Creek	5	4	137
48	Middle Santeetlah	5	4.25	126
51	Cheoah	5	4.5	128
54	Tellico Ledges	5	4.5	132
45	Upper Snowbird	5	4.75	122
52	Slickrock	5	4.75	130
50	Yellow Creek	5	5	127
47	Upper Santeetlah	5	5.5	124
60	Goforth Creek	5	5.5	141
77	Pigeon	6	3	169
72	Cataloochee Creek	6	3.5	162
63	Little River (Smokies)	6	3.75	148
65	Tremont	6	4	151
71	Greenbriar	6	4	161
64	Lynn Camp Prong	6	4.25	150
76	Lower Big Creek	6	4.5	168
70	Ramsay Prong	6	5	160
74	Pigeon Dries	6	5	164
66	Alum Cave	6	5.5	152
73	Hurricane Creek	6	5.5	163
75	Upper Big Creek	6	5.5	166
68	Upper West Prong	6	5.75	156
69	Lower West Prong	6	5.75	158
67	Road Prong	6	6	154
78	Raven Fork	6	6	170
80	Section IX	7	3.5	176
81	Big Laurel	7	3.75	178
84	Nolichucky	7	3.75	180
82	Spring Creek	7	4	179
79	Brush Creek	7	4.75	175
89	Upper Watauga	8	3	189
97	Lost Cove Creek	8	3.5	206
98	North Harper Creek	8	4.25	207
88	Red Roof of Watauga	8	4.5	188
94	Doe Gorge	8	4.5	197
99	Wilson Creek	8	4.5	208
90	Watauga Gorge	8	4.75	190
91	Upper Elk	8	5.25	192
96	Gragg Prong	8	5.25	204
92	Twisting Falls	8	5.5	194
93	Laurel Fork	8	5.5	196
95	Linville	8	5.5	198

Drainage areas for all of the free-flowing streams in the book are listed here, first by regions and then overall. Generally, rivers with smaller drainage areas have smaller river beds, and—assuming even rainfall over the entire area—require more rain to run, and drop out more quickly after the rain stops. Rivers with larger drainage areas often need less rainfall to get them going, and are more likely to be too high to run after a very heavy rainfall. If you arrive at a river and find it too high, either chill out and wait for the water to drop, or use this table to find a nearby river of comparable difficulty with a smaller drainage. If the water is too low, look for another nearby river with a larger drainage and try that out.

Reach#	River	Reg.	Drain.	Diff.	Pg.
8	North Pacolet	1	9	5	47
5	Big Hungry	1	19.3	4.5	41
1	Upper Rocky Broad	1	23	5	36
9	Dupont	1	32.9	5.75	48
3	Green River Dries	1	42.4	4.75	39
2	Rocky Broad	1	64.4	5.5	37
16	Big East Fork	2	1.2	5.5	60
17	Upper West Fork Pigeon	2	1.7	5.25	62
21	Bathtubs	2	1.8	5.25	66
12	Courthouse Creek	2	2.6	4.75	55
18	Garden of the Gods	2	5	6.25	63
20	Middle Prong	2	6.6	5.5	65
11	Looking Glass Creek	2	6.9	5	52
19	West Fork Pigeon	2	7.4	5.25	64
10	Upper Davidson	2	11.2	3.5	51
13	Upper NF French Broad	2	14.4	4.5	55
15	West Fork French Broad	2	18.8	4.75	58
14	North Fork French Broad	2	31.2	4.5	56
25	Silver Run Falls	3	2.4	5.75	77
28	Overflow	3	4.8	5.25	86
26	Upper Whitewater	3	4.9	5.5	78
22	Eastatoe	3	6.5	4.75	69
23	Toxaway	3	8	5.75	72
33	Upper Cullasaja	3	14.1	5.5	98
34	Middle Cullasaja	3	24.6	4.75	99
24	Horsepasture	3	25	5.75	74
35	Lower Cullasaja	3	34.1	5.75	100
27	Chauga	3	37.2	4.5	83
29	Section II	3	66.5	2	87
30	Section III	3	171	3.5	88
31	Section IV	3	203.1	4.75	90
40	Whiteoak Creek	4	13.8	5.5	110
41	Cascades	4	15.2	4.75	111
42	Upper Nantahala	4	15.4	3.5	113
39	Little Tennessee	4	439.4	2	109
45	Upper Snowbird	5	3.2	4.75	122
60	Goforth Creek	5	4	5.5	141
47	Upper Santeetlah	5	4.7	5.5	124
52	Slickrock	5	8.6	4.75	130
48	Middle Santeetlah	5	11.8	4.25	126
50	Yellow Creek	5	12.6	5	127
46	Lower Snowbird	5	12.7	4	123
53	Citico Creek	5	17.9	4	131
56	Coker Creek	5	19.3	4	137
49	Lower Santeetlah	5	20.1	3.5	126
54	Tellico Ledges	5	50.8	4.5	132
55	Middle Tellico	5	73.6	3.75	134
67	Road Prong	6	2	6	154
64	Lynn Camp Prong	6	5.6	4.25	150
66	Alum Cave	6	6.5	5.5	152
73	Hurricane Creek	6	8.4	5.5	163
68	Upper West Prong	6	12.6	5.75	156
69	Lower West Prong	6	14.4	5.75	158
70	Ramsay Prong	6	18.2	5	160
78	Raven Fork	6	19.5	6	170
65	Tremont	6	21.1	4	151
75	Upper Big Creek	6	23.1	5.5	166
76	Lower Big Creek	6	29.4	4.5	168
71	Greenbriar	6	37.7	4	161
72	Cataloochee Creek	6	49.3	3.5	162
63	Little River (Smokies)	6	53.1	3.75	148
79	Brush Creek	7	7.9	4.75	175
82	Spring Creek	7	60.9	4	179
81	Big Laurel	7	128.7	3.75	178
84	Nolichucky	7	607.8	3.75	180
80	Section IX	7	1368	3.5	176
98	North Harper Creek	8	4	4.25	207
96	Gragg Prong	8	5.1	5.25	204
97	Lost Cove Creek	8	5.4	3.5	206
91	Upper Elk	8	19.3	5.25	192
93	Laurel Fork	8	20	5.5	196
88	Red Roof of Watauga	8	22	4.5	188
95	Linville	8	44.4	5.75	198
92	Twisting Falls	8	44.9	5.5	194
94	Doe Gorge	8	60.4	4.5	197
99	Wilson Creek	8	60.9	4.5	208
89	Upper Watauga	8	93.8	3	189
90	Watauga Gorge	8	127.1	4.75	190

Reach#	River	Reg.	Drain.	Diff.	Pg.
16	Big East Fork	2	1.2	5.5	60
17	Upper West Fork Pigeon	2	1.7	5.25	62
21	Bathtubs	2	1.8	5.25	66
67	Road Prong	6	2	6	154
25	Silver Run Falls	3	2.4	5.75	77
12	Courthouse Creek	2	2.6	4.75	55
45	Upper Snowbird	5	3.2	4.75	122
60	Goforth Creek	5	4	5.5	141
98	North Harper Creek	8	4	4.25	207
47	Upper Santeetlah	5	4.7	5.5	124
28	Overflow	3	4.8	5.25	86
26	Upper Whitewater	3	4.9	5.5	78
18	Garden of the Gods	2	5	6.25	63
96	Gragg Prong	8	5.1	5.25	204
97	Lost Cove Creek	8	5.4	3.5	206
64	Lynn Camp Prong	6	5.6	4.25	150
22	Eastatoe	3	6.5	4.75	69
66	Alum Cave	6	6.5	5.5	152
20	Middle Prong	2	6.6	5.5	65
11	Looking Glass Creek	2	6.9	5	52
19	West Fork Pigeon	2	7.4	5.25	64
79	Brush Creek	7	7.9	4.75	175
23	Toxaway	3	8	5.75	72
73	Hurricane Creek	6	8.4	5.5	163
52	Slickrock	5	8.6	4.75	130
8	North Pacolet	1	9	5	47
10	Upper Davidson	2	11.2	3.5	51
48	Middle Santeetlah	5	11.8	4.25	126
50	Yellow Creek	5	12.6	5	127
68	Upper West Prong	6	12.6	5.75	156
46	Lower Snowbird	5	12.7	4	123
40	Whiteoak Creek	4	13.8	5.5	110
33	Upper Cullasaja	3	14.1	5.5	98
13	Upper NF French Broad	2	14.4	4.5	55
69	Lower West Prong	6	14.4	5.75	158
41	Cascades	4	15.2	4.75	111
42	Upper Nantahala	4	15.4	3.5	113
53	Citico Creek	5	17.9	4	131
70	Ramsay Prong	6	18.2	5	160

Reach#	River	Reg.	Drain.	Diff.	Pg.
15	West Fork French Broad	2	18.8	4.75	58
5	Big Hungry	1	19.3	4.5	41
56	Coker Creek	5	19.3	4	137
91	Upper Elk	8	19.3	5.25	192
78	Raven Fork	6	19.5	6	170
93	Laurel Fork	8	20	5.5	196
49	Lower Santeetlah	5	20.1	3.5	126
65	Tremont	6	21.1	4	151
88	Red Roof of Watauga	8	22	4.5	188
1	Upper Rocky Broad	1	23	5	36
75	Upper Big Creek	6	23.1	5.5	166
34	Middle Cullasaja	3	24.6	4.75	99
24	Horsepasture	3	25	5.75	74
76	Lower Big Creek	6	29.4	4.5	168
14	North Fork French Broad	2	31.2	4.5	56
9	Dupont	1	32.9	5.75	48
35	Lower Cullasaja	3	34.1	5.75	100
27	Chauga	3	37.2	4.5	83
71	Greenbrier	6	37.7	4	161
3	Green River Dries	1	42.4	4.75	39
95	Linville	8	44.4	5.75	198
92	Twisting Falls	8	44.9	5.5	194
72	Cataloochee Creek	6	49.3	3.5	162
54	Tellico Ledges	5	50.8	4.5	132
63	Little River (Smokies)	6	53.1	3.75	148
94	Doe Gorge	8	60.4	4.5	197
82	Spring Creek	7	60.9	4	179
99	Wilson Creek	8	60.9	4.5	208
2	Rocky Broad	1	64.4	5.5	37
29	Section II	3	66.5	2	87
55	Middle Tellico	5	73.6	3.75	134
89	Upper Watauga	8	93.8	3	189
90	Watauga Gorge	8	127.1	4.75	190
81	Big Laurel	7	128.7	3.75	178
30	Section III	3	171	3.5	88
31	Section IV	3	203.1	4.75	90
39	Little Tennessee	4	439.4	2	109
84	Nolichucky	7	607.8	3.75	180
80	Section IX	7	1368	3.5	176

· COMMON DIRECTIONS & SHORT-CUTS FROM ASHEVILLE ·

Asheville to the 64/276/280 junction at Pisgah Forest: Take I-26 East to exit 40. Take exit 40, and make a right at the light on 280 West. Continue 16 miles to the junction.

Asheville to the 64/215 junction at Rosman: Follow the above directions to Pisgah Forest and continue straight through the light at the junction on 64 West. Follow 64 2.9 miles into Brevard to a light just across from Brevard College. Bear right through this light on business 64 and follow the road through downtown 1 mile until it runs back into 64. Make a right on 64 West, and continue a little over 8 miles to the 64/215 junction at Headwaters Outfitters.

Asheville to the Forks of the Pigeon: Take I-40 West to exit 37 (East Canton Exit). Make a left at the bottom of the ramp, and a right at the light on 19/23. Take 19/23 over 4 miles until you see the Hot Spot station on the left. Shortly after the Hot Spot, make a left at the funeral home. Bear right at the end of the funeral home (watch your speed—sometimes police hang out in the back parking lot), go up the hill, and continue to the double enforced stop sign. Make a right at the sign, and then an immediate left. A short distance later, bear right in front of the stone arch at the cemetery, continue past the swimming pool hand rail (at the cemetery—there is no pool), and skirt the cemetery until you head down the hill. At the stop sign, go straight onto highway 110. Go about 5 miles to the light at the 276/215/110 junction.

For the Big East Fork: Make a left on 276 at the light, and go 11.5 miles to the Big East Fork trailhead on the right.

For the West Fork, Middle Prong, and The Bathtubs: Go straight through the light on 215 at the 276/215/110 junction. Go until the stop sign and make a left to stay on 215 South. Follow 215 South about 2 miles to the turn for the Bathtubs, or continue on 215 past Lake Logan to the Sunburst Rec Area and the West Fork and Middle Prong.

Asheville to the Chauga, Chattooga Sections II and III, and Overflow: Take I-26 East to Exit 54. Follow the connector from Exit 54 until it turns into US 25, and continue into South Carolina 7 miles to SC 11. Make a left just after going under the bridge, proceed up the ramp, and make another left on SC 11 heading West. Go a little over 4 miles, and make a right at the T junction in Cleveland to stay on SC 11. Go another 5.4 miles, and make a left to stay on 11 at the 11/276 junction

(enjoying the view of Table Rock, SC). After about 32 more miles, you will see the sign for the town of Picket Post. There will be a road to the right with a brown sign for Oconee Station. Skip this turn, and take the next right on Picket Post Rd. Follow Picket Post 3.8 miles to a stop sign at a complicated junction. Go right on the larger of the two right roads—the less sharp turn (although still more than 90 degrees). Go a little over 2 miles to a right turn just past a house with a swimming pool and a white picket fence. Follow the short road to a right turn on highway 28. Follow 28 North 3.2 miles to a left turn on Whetstone Road.

For the Chauga: take Whetstone 3/4 mile to a left on Cassidy Bridge Road, and follow that 5 miles to the put in.

For the Chattooga: take Whetstone Road just under 5 miles to Chattooga Ridge Road. Go straight on Earl's Ford Road for the Earl's Ford or Sandy Ford access points, or make a left on Chattooga Ridge and continue to a right on US 76 to the bridge.

For Overflow: Continue north on 28 to the bridge over the Chattooga and follow the reach directions from there.

Asheville to the Cullasaja, Tallulah, or Chattooga Section IV:

NOTE: If you are coming from the south side of Asheville, the above directions to the Chauga and Sections II and III will be a faster way to reach the 76 bridge and Section IV.

Take I-40 West to exit 27 (Clyde exit). Take US 74/23 through Waynesville, and continue to Sylva. Just past Sylva, look for the US 441 South exit to Dillsboro/Franklin/Atlanta. Take 441 South to Franklin, where you will stay straight on the 441 bypass.

For the Cullasaja: Look for the 64 East exit from the 441 bypass, and take 64 East to the Cullasaja Gorge.

For Tallulah and Section IV: After crossing the Cullasaja and Little Tennessee Rivers, be on the lookout for an exit to 441 South. Take this exit, and continue south to Clayton, GA.

For the Tallulah: Continue south on 441 from Clayton to the obvious boater parking area just after the bridge at the dam after Tallulah Falls State Park.

For Section IV: Make a left on US 76 in Clayton, and go about 8 miles to the bridge.

Region 4 - The Central Mountains

Asheville to Cullowhee: Take I-40 West to exit 27 (Clyde exit). Take US 74/23 through Waynesville, and continue to Sylva. Take the first Sylva exit, and go to the T junction with 107. Make a left on 107 and follow it a few miles to Cullowhee.

Asheville to Wesser: Take I-40 West to exit 27 (Clyde exit). Take US 74/23 through Waynesville, and continue past Sylva and Bryson City to the Capt. TA Sandlin Bridge over the Little Tennessee/Fontana Lake. A little over 2 miles past the bridge, bear left on US 19. Follow 19 a little over 4 miles to the NOC in Wesser.

Region 5 - The Western Mountains

Asheville to Robbinsville: Take I-40 West to exit 27 (Clyde exit). Take US 74/23 through Waynesville, and continue past Sylva and Bryson City to the Capt. TA Sandlin Bridge over the Little Tennessee/Fontana Lake. A little over 2 miles past the bridge, bear right on highway 28. Go about 11.5 miles, and make a left turn on 143. Follow 143 over Stecoah Gap and down into Robbinsville. Make a right at the light on US 129 and the Texaco/Subway will be obvious on the right.

Asheville to Tellico Plains: Follow the above directions to Robbinsville. Head north on 129 1.4 miles to a left turn signed to Joyce Kilmer and the Cherohala Skyway. Follow this road about 3.4 miles until it ends, and turn right onto NC 1127. Continue a little over 6.5 miles to Santeetlah Gap, going straight to get on the Cherohala Skyway. Take the Skyway over the mountain and into Tellico Plains.

Asheville to the Ocoee: Take I-40 West to exit 27 (Clyde exit). Take US 74/23 through Waynesville, and continue past Sylva and Bryson City to the Capt. TA Sandlin Bridge over the Little Tennessee/Fontana Lake. A little over 2 miles past the bridge, bear left on US 19. Follow 19 through the Nantahala Gorge and continue through Andrews to Murphy. In Murphy, US 64 joins with 19. Follow 64 West to the Ocoee.

Region 6 - The Smokies

Asheville to Newfound Gap: Take I-40 West to exit 27 (Clyde exit). Take US 74/23 through Waynesville, and continue past Sylva about 9.5 miles to the US 441 North / Cherokee Exit. Take the exit and follow the road north until it ends. Go right, and make a left at the light after a short distance back onto 441 North.

Follow 441 North through Cherokee and into the National Park, continuing to Newfound Gap at the top of the mountain.

Asheville to the Little River: Follow the above directions to Newfound Gap, and continue down the hill into Tennessee on 441. At the Sugarlands Ranger Station, make a left on highway 73, which leads down the Little River and into Townsend.

Asheville to Gatlinburg: Follow the above directions to Newfound Gap, and continue down the hill on 441 and into Gatlinburg.

Region 8 - The Northern Mountains

Asheville to Hampton, TN: Take I-26 West past Erwin, TN. Take Exit 23 (Unicoi Exit). Make a right at the bottom of the ramp, and a right on 173 toward the town of Unicoi. Make a left in the town of Unicoi onto 107, and continue about .7 miles to a left on Scioto Road. Follow Scioto Road until it ends, and make a right on 361. Follow this road until it ends, and make another right (at the old stone school house) to stay on 361. Continue to the T junction at US 19E. Make a left and continue to the Shell/Subway at the US 321 Junction in Hampton.

Asheville to Elk Park and Banner Elk: Take I-26 West past Erwin, TN. Take Exit 23 (Unicoi Exit). Make a right at the bottom of the ramp, and a right on 173 toward the town of Unicoi. Make a left in the town of Unicoi onto 107, and continue about .7 miles to a left on Scioto Road. Follow Scioto Road until it ends, and make a right on 361. Follow this road until it ends, and make another right (at the old stone school house) to stay on 361. Continue to the T junction at US 19E. Make a right on 19E, and follow it over the hill through Roan Mountain and into Elk Park. Take 194 East out of Elk Park to reach Banner Elk.

Asheville to the Watauga Gorge: Follow the above directions to Hampton, TN. From Hampton, head east on 321 past Watauga Lake to the NC state line, and follow the reach directions from there.

Asheville to Wilson Creek/Brown Mountain Beach: Take I-40 East to exit 100. Make a left at the end of the ramp, and continue until the road ends at the Eckerd's Drug store just past Freedom High School. Make a left on highway 181, and continue about 10 miles to Brown Mountain Beach Road on the right—just before a white church. Take Brown Mountain Beach Road about 5 miles to the bridge over Wilson Creek. Just after the bridge, make a left and continue into the gorge to Brown Mountain Beach.

· FROM THE AUTHOR ·

I came to paddling from the sport of climbing—excited to try a new mode of exploration, and thrilled by the dreams of all the new and incredible adventures that awaited me in the river valleys and gorges of Western North Carolina. I had a feeling of the scale and the thrill of outdoor sports, but no idea as to what a real whitewater adventure would be like. I moved to the Asheville area and set about the decade-long process of turning that mass of dreams into a story book of memories—which have become a large part of who I am. To some extent that's what NCRC is—a catalogue of my memories of the rivers of this area. However, what I have written is not meant to be a story book of my adventures—it is a tool to help you go out and turn your paddling dreams into your own story book of river trips.

Over the last few years I've traveled back and forth across this continent many times, exploring rivers everywhere I've gone. I own a lot of guidebooks, and I have used most of them at one time or another. They are invaluable tools to the traveling paddler—the insight of a local in the hands of a wanderer in a strange land. I hope that folks traveling to this area will add NCRC to their library and will find it to be a good tool for exploring the wonders of this region. For those of you who are buying this as the guidebook to your home paddling area, I urge you not to let this be the only paddling guide you own. There are lots of good ones out there. Pick a spot that you've always dreamed of boating, get online, and buy the guide to that area. The more time you spend reading that guide, the more likely it is that you will some day transform your dreams of traveling to that area into memories of the trip of a lifetime.

locust fork, alabama, 1988   bull sluice, chattooga, 1993   zwick's backender, green narrows, 1995   sinks of the little, 2005

NCRC author evolves over the years as a paddler: shorter boat, longer paddle, shorter hair, bigger gut.

· ABOUT THE AUTHOR ·

Born in New Orleans in 1972, Leland spent most of his time from 1981 onward longing for his summer trips to camp in Western North Carolina's Green River Drainage, and for paddling and climbing trips with his high school outdoor program. He first sunk his paddle in the Green River from the seat of a tandem canoe on the Lower Green in the summer of '82. In 1990 he moved from New Orleans to Colorado to pursue his passion for rock climbing, but still got in annual trips to NC to paddle the solo open canoe he received as his high school graduation present. In '93, after seeing the video "Green Summer" in Utah, he moved permanently to the Asheville area where he bought a C-1 and has been paddling ever since. In 1998 he cut off his lustrous

mullet, got a two bladed paddle, and took to butt boating. To support his habit he has been a camp counselor, outdoor guide, run high adventure and university programs, been a dish washer, waiter, valet, painter, videographer, graphic designer, sales rep, freelance writer, and pumpkin salesman. He has worked in the paddling industry for Savage Designs, Watershed, Stahlsac, Pothole Paddles, Impex, Pyranha, and Astral Buoyancy. Today he lives on a mountain outside of Swannanoa, NC—where he and his girlfriend/paddling-partner Andria have a small publishing company—Brushy Mountain Publishing—which creates books and DVDs. Look for them anywhere on the planet that rocks, water, gravity and gradient are found together in abundance.

• COLOPHON •

AUTHOR

Software
Text: SimpleText and MS Word X for Mac
Beta: MS Excel X for Mac, National Geographic Topo!
Maps: National Geographic Topo! and Adobe Photoshop CS
Photo Post Processing: Adobe Photoshop CS

Hardware
Writing and photo processing:
-Power Mac G4 Dual 450 mhz with 1 GB RAM
-Power Mac G5 Dual 1.8 ghz with 2 GB RAM

Photo Scanning:
Photos scanned to PM G4 Dual 450 mhz using:
-Polaroid SprintScan35
-UMAX Astra 2400S

Photography:
All of the author's photos shot using:
-Nikon D70
-w/SimpleTech CompactFlash 1.0 GB
-Nikon N80
-Nikon N60
-Nikkor AF 35-80 f4-5.6D
-Nikkor ED AF 80-200 f2.8
-Nikkor AF 70-300 f4-5.6
-Fuji Provia 100F
-Fuji Provia 400F

LAYOUT

Software
The CS version of the Adobe Creative Suite was used for the book layout and was completed in approximately 5 months.

Hardware
The entire project and all associated files were kept on a 80GB LaCie external Firewire drive. That hard drive visited four western locations during the winter of 2004/05: Boulder, Colorado, Baja del Sur, Driggs, Idaho, and Nelson, British Columbia (whereever the surf or the powder was good). Thanx to all that allowed me to dock into their CPUs and borrow some processor cycles, otherwise, an Apple G4 1GHz CPU was used with a 20" Apple Cinema Screen.

Remote File Transfer
All files were shared with NCRC world headquarters in North Carolina via FTP and stored on a Mac OSX Server located in Boulder, Colorado.

Proofing
PDFs were generated from Adobe Indesign and printed at Kinkos with a Fiery Rip.

Typography
-Body text is Gill Sans Book
-Run title text is Lithos Pro
-Chapter title text is Charlemagne

Project Digital Size
-28GB
-180 line art drawings
- Emails from Leland: 495

Book Design
Gordon Banks
gordon@kayakingcolorado.com
http://www.kayakingcolorado.com/gordon/

· RUN INDEX ·